# A Doll's House

Henrik Ibsen (1828-1906). Norwegian poet and playwright. His plays include: *Peer Gynt* (1867), *A Doll's House* (1879), *Ghosts* (1881), *An Enemy of the People* (1882), *Hedda Gabler* (1890) and *The Master Builder* (1892).

Frank McGuinness was born in Buncrana, Co. Donegal, and now lives in Dublin and lectures in English at St Patrick's College, Maynooth. His plays include: *The Factory Girls* (Abbey Theatre, Dublin, 1984), *Baglady* (Abbey, 1985), *Observe the Sons of Ulster Marching Towards the Somme* (Abbey, 1985; Hampstead Theatre, London, 1986), *Innocence* (Gate Theatre, Dublin, 1986), *Carthaginians* (Abbey, 1988; Hampstead, 1989), *Mary and Lizzie* (RSC, 1989), *The Bread Man* (Gate, 1991), *Someone Who'll Watch Over Me* (Hampstead, West End and Broadway, 1992), *The Bird Sanctuary* (Abbey, 1994), *Mutabilitie* (National Theatre, 1997) and *Dolly West's Kitchen* (Abbey, 1999; Old Vic, London, 2000). His translations include Ibsen's *Rosmersholm* (RNT, 1987), *Peer Gynt* (Gate, 1988; RSC and international tour, 1994) and *Hedda Gabler* (Roundabout Theatre, Broadway, 1994); Chekhov's *Three Sisters* (Gate and Royal Court, 1990) and *Uncle Vanya* (Field Day production, 1995); Lorca's *Yerma* (Abbey, 1987); Brecht's *The Threepenny Opera* (Gate, 1991); and Ostrovsky's *The Storm* (Almeida, 1998).

# HENRIK IBSEN

# A Doll's House

*in a new version*
*by Frank McGuinness*

*from a literal translation*
*by Charlotte Barslund*

*faber and faber*
LONDON·NEW YORK

For Catherine Bunyon and Thelma Holt

First published in 1996
by Faber and Faber Limited
3 Queen Square, London WCIN 3AU

First published in the United States in 1997
by Faber and Faber, Inc.
An affiliate of Farrar, Straus and Giroux
19 Union Square West, New York 10003

Typeset by Faber and Faber Ltd
Printed in the United States of America

A CIP record for this book
is available from the British Library

ISBN 0-571-19129-0

First U.S. printing, 2002

4   6   8   10   12   13   11   9   7   5

# Characters

Nora Helmer
Torvald Helmer
Mrs Linde
Krogstad
Doctor Rank
Bob and Ivan, children
Helene, maid
Messenger
Anne-Marie, nanny

**A Doll's House** was first produced by Thelma Holt at the Playhouse Theatre on 22 October 1996 with the following cast:

**Nora Helmer**  Janet McTeer
**Torvald Helmer**  Owen Teale
**Kristine Linde**  Gabrielle Lloyd
**Nils Krogstad**  Peter Gowen
**Dr Rank**  John Carlisle
**Anne-Marie**  Illona Linthwaite
**Helene**  Judith Hepburn
**Messenger**  Murray McArthur

*Directed by*  Anthony Page
*Designed by*  Deirdre Clancy
*Lighting by*  Peter Mumford
*Music by*  Jason Carr
*Sound by*  Scott Myers and John Owens
*Choreography by*  Caroline Pope

# Act One

A warm, well-furnished room, reflecting more taste than expense. At stage right, a door leads to a hall. Another door, stage left, leads to Helmer's study. There is a piano between these two doors. There is a door in the middle of the wall, stage left, and a window further downstage. There is a round table near the window, with armchairs and a small sofa. Somewhat towards the back in the side wall, stage right, there is a door, and further downstage on the same wall a stove covered in white tiles with a couple of armchairs and a rocking chair in front of it. Between the stove and the side door there is a small table. There are engravings on the walls. There is a what-not with china pieces and other little knick-knacks on it. There is a small bookcase with expensively bound books in it. The floor is carpeted, and there is a fire burning in the stove. It is a winter's day.

A bell rings in the hall and we hear the door open shortly afterwards. Nora enters the room, humming cheerfully to herself. She wears outdoor clothes and carries a number of packages. She puts them on the table, stage right. She has left open the door to the hall and we can see a Messenger carrying a Christmas tree. He has given a basket to the Maid, Helene, who opened the door to them.

**Nora** The Christmas tree, hide it away safely, Helene. Until this evening. The children can't see it until it's been decorated. (*She takes out her purse.*) How much –

**Messenger** Fifty øre.

I

**Nora**  A hundred, take it, keep it all.

*The Messenger thanks her and leaves. Nora closes the door. She keeps laughing, quietly, cheerfully, as she takes her coat off. She takes out the bag of macaroons from her pocket and eats a few. She then walks cautiously towards her husband's door and listens.*

Yes, he is at home.

*Nora hums again as she goes to the table stage right. Helmer calls from his study.*

**Helmer**  Is that skylark chirping out there, is that who's out there?

*Nora is busily opening some of the parcels.*

**Nora**  Yes, yes.

**Helmer**  Squirrel, squirrel, is that who's out there?

**Nora**  Yes, yes.

**Helmer**  When did squirrel scamper home?

**Nora**  Just now. (*She puts the bag of macaroons in her pocket and wipes her mouth.*) Torvald, come here and see what I've bought.

**Helmer**  I can't be disturbed. (*After a while he opens the door, looks out, pen in hand.*) Did you say bought? All of this? I've a little bird who likes to fritter money, has that little bird been frittering again?

**Nora**  Yes, but this year, Torvald, we can spend a little more. This is the first Christmas we've not had to watch the purse strings.

**Helmer**  You know very well we can't spend a fortune.

**Nora**  I said a little more, Torvald. We can, yes? Just a little more! You're going to get a big salary and you will earn pots and pots of money.

**Helmer** After the New Year, yes, but it will be a full three months before the salary is due.

**Nora** So? So? We can borrow till then.

**Helmer** Nora! (*He goes and playfully pinches her ear.*) Are you being a silly girl? Say I borrowed a thousand and you let it slip through your fingers during Christmas, and then a tile falls off the roof, hits me on the head and flattens me.

*Nora puts her hand over his mouth.*

**Nora** Stop it. Don't say such horrible things.

**Helmer** But just say something horrible happened – what then?

**Nora** If something that horrible did happen, it wouldn't matter if I had debts or not.

**Helmer** What about the people I've borrowed from?

**Nora** Them? They're strangers. Who cares about strangers?

**Helmer** Nora, my Nora, that is just like a woman. Now, be serious, Nora. You know what I think. No debts, no borrowing – never. A home that depends on loans and debts is not beautiful because it is not free. Look, the two of us have managed well enough up to now. We still have to manage for a short while, and we will, because we must.

*Nora goes towards the stove.*

**Nora** Everything as you wish, Torvald.

*He follows her.*

**Helmer** Who's hanging her head, is it my little skylark?

She mustn't. Who's sulking, is it my squirrel? Is it? (*He takes out his wallet.*) Nora, look, what have I here?

*Nora turns briskly.*

**Nora**  Money!

**Helmer**  Yes. (*He hands her some notes.*) I know how much money needs to be spent in a house at Christmas.

*Nora counts.*

**Nora**  Ten – twenty – thirty – forty. Torvald, thank you. I will stretch it out, thank you.

**Helmer**  Yes, do that. You must do that.

**Nora**  Yes, I promise. Come on, I've got to show you what I've bought. For virtually nothing. New clothes here for Ivan – and a sword. A horse for Bob, and here, a trumpet. A doll and a cradle for Emmy. Nothing much! She'll soon rip it to ribbons anyway. I got some material for the maids – make dresses and scarves. Old Anne-Marie should get something better really.

**Helmer**  What lurks in that particular parcel?

*Nora screams.*

**Nora**  No, Torvald, you're not to see that until this evening.

**Helmer**  I see. What have you dreamt up for yourself? Well, tell me, you little spendthrift?

**Nora**  For me? Nothing. I want nothing.

**Helmer**  You most certainly do. Tell me what you'd like – something sensible.

**Nora**  I don't know. Yes, I do. Torvald, listen to me.

**Helmer**  What?

*Without looking at him, Nora fingers his buttons.*

**Nora** If you want to give me something, could you – could you –

**Helmer** Say it, say it.

**Nora** Money. Give me money, Torvald. As much as you think you can spare. I can buy something with it one of these days.

**Helmer** No, Nora, really –

**Nora** Please, dear Torvald, do that. I've asked you so sweetly. I would hang the money on the Christmas tree, wrapped in beautiful gold paper. That would be fun, wouldn't it?

**Helmer** There are little birds that like to fritter money. What do you call them?

**Nora** Little fritter birds, yes, I know them well. Let's do as I say, Torvald. I'll take time to think what I need most. That would be sensible, yes? What do you say?

*Helmer smiles.*

**Helmer** Sensible, yes. If you could only hold on to my money and buy something you really need. But it goes on the house and so many useless odds and ends and then I've to put my hand into my wallet all over again.

**Nora** But Torvald –

**Helmer** But nothing, my lovely, little Nora. (*He puts his arms around her waist.*) My little bird that fritters is so very fragile, but she does waste an awful lot of money. Who would believe how much it costs to keep that little bird?

**Nora** How can you say that? I do try to save up all that I can.

*Helmer laughs.*

**Helmer** You do, you do. All that you can. But you can't.

*Nora turns and smiles, quietly pleased.*

**Nora** Torvald, if you only knew how many expenses singing birds and squirrels have.

**Helmer** You're a strange little creature. So like your father. You try every trick to get money. When you do get it, it disappears through your fingers. You never know how you spent it. Well, I have to take you as you are.

**Nora** I wish I were more like my Papa.

**Helmer** But I wouldn't want you any other way. Stay as you are, my lovely little singing bird. But you, Nora, you look quite . . . quite . . . devious today –

**Nora** I do?

**Helmer** You do, yes. Look into my eyes.

*Nora looks at him.*

**Nora** What?

*Helmer wags his finger.*

**Helmer** Was a sweet tooth indulged in town today by any chance?

**Nora** No, what are you thinking?

**Helmer** Did a sweet tooth stroll into a pastry shop?

**Nora** No, I swear it, Torvald –

**Helmer** Gobble up a little jam?

**Nora** Absolutely not.

**Helmer** Helped itself to a macaroon or two?

**Nora**  No, Torvald, I really swear it –

**Helmer**  All right! You know, I'm only joking –

*Nora goes to the table, stage right.*

**Nora**  You told me not to, do you think I'd –

**Helmer**  No, I know that very well. You've given me your word. So, my dearest Nora, keep your little festive secrets all to yourself. We will know all when the Christmas tree is lit.

**Nora**  Did you remember to invite Doctor Rank?

**Helmer**  No need to. He'll dine with us. Goes without saying. Anyway, he'll call here this morning. I can ask him then. I have ordered wonderful wines. Nora, you can't imagine how much I'm looking forward to this evening.

**Nora**  Me too. The children will really enjoy it as well, Torvald.

**Helmer**  It is so good to know that one has a secure, respectable position. And an ample salary. Isn't that so? It is a great pleasure to know that, yes?

**Nora**  Yes, it is marvellous!

**Helmer**  Do you remember last Christmas? Three whole weeks you buried yourself away, every night after midnight, making flowers for the Christmas tree and all the other surprises. (*He shudders.*) I have never been more bored.

**Nora**  I wasn't bored at all.

*Helmer smiles.*

**Helmer**  But it didn't work out all that well, did it?

**Nora**  Don't tease me about that. Was it my fault the cat got in and tore everything to pieces?

**Helmer** No, of course it wasn't, my poor little Nora. You wanted us all to be happy, and that's what matters. Still, it's good those hard times are gone.

**Nora** Yes, yes, it's marvellous.

**Helmer** Now I no longer have to sit alone and bore myself. You don't have to hurt your lovely eyes and your delicate, frail hands –

*Nora claps her hands.*

**Nora** No, that's so, Torvald, no need for any more of that. How marvellous it is to know that. (*She takes him by the arm.*) Now listen, Torvald, I want to tell you how I think we can arrange things. Once Christmas is over –

*A bell rings in the hallway.*

**Helmer** The door bell.

*Nora tidies up a little in the living room.*

I'm not at home. Remember that.

*The Maid stands in the hall doorway.*

**Maid** Mrs Helmer, there is a lady here – a stranger.

**Nora** Show her in.

**Maid** The doctor's arrived at the same time.

**Helmer** Did he go straight into my study?

**Maid** He did.

*Helmer enters the study. The Maid shows Mrs Linde into the room and closes the door behind her. Mrs Linde is dressed in travelling clothes. She speaks timidly and a little reluctantly.*

**Mrs Linde** Nora, hello.

*Nora is uncertain.*

**Nora** Hello –

**Mrs Linde** Oh, you don't recognize me.

**Nora** No, I'm not sure – yes, I think it's – (*She cries out.*) What! Kristine! Is it really you?

**Mrs Linde** Yes, it is me.

**Nora** Kristine! I did not recognize you. I didn't. How could I – (*She speaks more quietly.*) Kristine, you've changed so much.

**Mrs Linde** I believe I have, yes. Nine, ten years, long years.

**Nora** Is it that long since we last saw each other? It is, so it is. I've been so happy these last eight years. And now have you come to town? Did you make that long journey in winter? How brave of you.

**Mrs Linde** I arrived on the steamer this morning.

**Nora** For Christmas, of course, to have a good time. How lovely. We will have such fun. Come on, take off your coat. Oh, you're freezing. (*She helps Mrs Linde.*) Now, sit down by the warm stove. No, in that armchair. I'll take the rocking chair. (*She clasps Mrs Linde's hands.*) Yes, you're now looking like you used to look. It was just at first – you do look paler, Kristine, and perhaps a little thinner.

**Mrs Linde** And older, Nora, much older.

**Nora** A little older, yes, perhaps, a tiny little bit. Not much, not much. (*She stops suddenly and looks serious.*) I am so thoughtless, sitting here chattering. Dear, good Kristine, can you forgive me?

**Mrs Linde** Forgive you? Why, Nora?

*Nora replies quietly.*

**Nora** Poor Kristine, you lost your husband.

**Mrs Linde** Three years ago, yes.

**Nora** I heard about it. I read it in the newspapers. Kristine, do believe me, I meant so often to write to you then, but I kept putting it off and something always got in the way.

**Mrs Linde** My dear Nora, I understand perfectly.

**Nora** No, it was bad of me, Kristine. You poor woman, you've gone through so much. He didn't leave you anything to live on?

**Mrs Linde** Nothing.

**Nora** And no children?

**Mrs Linde** None.

**Nora** Nothing at all then?

**Mrs Linde** He left me nothing, not even an ounce of grief.

*Nora looks at her in disbelief.*

**Nora** Kristine, can that be possible?

*Mrs Linde smiles sadly and strokes Nora's hair.*

**Mrs Linde** That does happen sometimes, Nora.

**Nora** You're alone then. Alone. That must be very difficult for you. I have three such lovely children. You can't see them just yet. The nanny's taken them out. But tell me everything –

**Mrs Linde** No, no, no, you talk to me.

**Nora** You start. Please. I won't be selfish today. Today I will think only about you. But I do have to tell you one thing. Have you heard our wonderful news?

**Mrs Linde** No, what?

**Nora** Imagine it, my husband has been appointed manager of the New Savings Bank.

**Mrs Linde** Your husband – that is lucky –

**Nora** Yes – very. Being a lawyer is such an insecure life, especially if you don't want to touch any case that is not honourable and above board. Torvald naturally never wanted to do anything else, and I totally agree with him there. Oh, believe me, we are so happy. After the New Year he starts work at the bank and he will get a large salary with a fair share of bonuses. From then on we can live quite differently. We can do as we like. Kristine, I feel so happy and free. It is gorgeous to have pots and pots of money and never have to worry. Isn't it?

**Mrs Linde** Yes indeed, it must be lovely to have the basics.

**Nora** More than the basics, pots and pots of money.

*Mrs Linde smiles.*

**Mrs Linde** Nora, Nora, haven't you got any sense yet? Even in school you spent money like water.

*Nora laughs quietly.*

**Nora** I know, and Torvald says I still do. (*She wags her finger.*) But 'Nora, Nora' is not as scatty as you think. Our life has not been that easy. We've had very little money. Nothing to waste. We have both had to work hard.

**Mrs Linde** You as well?

**Nora** Yes. Bits and pieces. Needlework, crocheting, embroidery – stuff like that. (*She adds casually:*) Other things as well. Did you know Torvald left the Civil Service when we married? There wasn't any chance of promotion in his office, and he had to earn more money than before.

But in that first year he worked his fingers down to the bone. He had to find all sorts of extra work. You can't imagine how hard he was working, from morning to night. He couldn't take it and he became so ill – so very, very ill. The doctors told me it was absolutely necessary that he travelled south.

**Mrs Linde** You spent an entire year in Italy, didn't you?

**Nora** We did. It was hard to get away, believe me. Ivan had just been born. But we did really have to go. And it saved his life, Torvald's life. It was a wonderful year. It did cost an awful lot of money, Kristine.

**Mrs Linde** I would imagine so.

**Nora** Four thousand eight hundred crowns – a lot – a lot of money.

**Mrs Linde** You were very lucky that you had it for such an emergency.

**Nora** We got it from Papa, you know.

**Mrs Linde** I see. It was around the time your father died.

**Nora** Yes, Kristine. That's when it was. And can you imagine, I couldn't go to nurse him. I was stuck here, expecting Ivan to be born any day. I also had Torvald to look after, and he was ill, so very ill. My Papa, so dear, so kind – I never saw him again, Kristine. That's the worst thing that's happened to me since I married.

**Mrs Linde** I know how fond you were of him. So then you left for Italy?

**Nora** Yes, we had the money by then. The doctors insisted. So we left a month later.

**Mrs Linde** And your husband came back in good health?

**Nora** Fit as a fiddle.

**Mrs Linde** But – the doctor?

**Nora** I'm sorry?

**Mrs Linde** I thought the maid said it was the doctor – the gentleman who arrived at the same time as me?

**Nora** Doctor Rank, yes. But this isn't a professional visit. He's our closest friend. He drops by at least once a day. No, Torvald has not been ill for one moment since then. And the children are well, they're healthy, and I am too. (*She jumps up and claps her hands.*) Oh God, Kristine, it is so wonderful to be alive and to be happy. Oh, how horrible of me – rabbiting on about me and me and me. (*She sits down on a footstool close by Mrs Linde and puts her arms on Mrs Linde's knees.*) Don't be angry with me, don't. Tell me, is it really true that you didn't love your husband? Why did you marry him? Tell me.

**Mrs Linde** My mother was alive then. She was bed-ridden. Helpless. I had two younger brothers. I had to take care of them. I could not refuse his offer. It wouldn't have been justifiable.

**Nora** No, I suppose you're right, it wouldn't have. So was he rich?

**Mrs Linde** He did have money, but the whole business was shaky. Then he died, and everything collapsed. There was nothing left.

**Nora** What happened?

**Mrs Linde** I had to manage a little shop then. And a little school. And anything else I could think of. These last three years, they've passed like one long working day, working – I've had no rest. It is over now, Nora. My poor mother's died, she doesn't need me. The boys don't either. They've found positions, they can look after themselves.

13

**Nora** You must feel so relieved –

**Mrs Linde** Empty. I cannot tell you how empty. No one to live for any more. (*She gets up uneasily.*) That's why I couldn't stay there a moment longer in that remote place. Better to find something here to occupy me, that will make demands on me. If I could only find a job, some office job –

**Nora** Kristine, no, it will wear you out and you look so exhausted already. Why don't you go to a spa –

*Mrs Linde goes to the window.*

**Mrs Linde** Nora, I do not have a Papa to give me money to travel.

**Nora** Don't be cross with me, don't.

*Mrs Linde goes to her.*

**Mrs Linde** Nora, don't you be cross with me. When you're in my position, you become bitter, and that is the worst thing possible. You have no one to work for, but you have to look out for yourself all the time. You have to survive and then you get selfish. Can you believe this? When you told me of your good news I was happy not for your sake, but for my own.

**Nora** Why? I understand. You think Torvald might be able to do something to help you.

**Mrs Linde** Yes, I do think that.

**Nora** Well, he will, Kristine. Leave it to me. I will come round to it when the time is right, and the time will be right. I'll think of something he really likes. And I would truly like to be able to help you.

**Mrs Linde** Nora, this is so kind of you, you want to help me – especially you who knows so little of how difficult life can be –

**Nora** I know – I know so little –

*Mrs Linde smiles.*

**Mrs Linde** Dear God, you do some needlework, you embroider – you are a child, Nora.

*Nora tosses her head and crosses the floor.*

**Nora** Don't say that to me, don't talk down to me.

**Mrs Linde** I'm sorry.

**Nora** You're as bad as the rest of them. You all think that I'm useless when it comes to knowing how hard life can be –

**Mrs Linde** No, no –

**Nora** You think I haven't been through anything difficult.

**Mrs Linde** Nora dear, you've just told me about your troubles.

**Nora** That was nothing. (*She speaks quietly.*) There's a big thing I've not told you.

**Mrs Linde** What do you mean?

**Nora** You look down on me, Kristine. You shouldn't. You're proud that you worked so long and hard for your mother.

**Mrs Linde** I do not look down on anyone. But it is true that I'm proud and happy I was allowed to give my mother peace in her dying years.

**Nora** You're also proud when you think of what you've done for your brothers.

**Mrs Linde** I think I am entitled to be.

**Nora** So do I. But listen to me, Kristine. I have something to be proud and happy about as well.

**Mrs Linde** I wouldn't doubt it. What?

**Nora** Keep your voice down. Torvald must not hear this. He must never hear this. No one must know, Kristine. No one but you.

**Mrs Linde** What is it?

**Nora** Come here. (*She pulls Mrs Linde down on the sofa beside her.*) Yes, I have something to be proud of, I have something to be happy about – I saved Torvald's life. I saved his life.

**Mrs Linde** Saved? How did you save –

**Nora** The trip to Italy I told you about, Torvald would be dead if he hadn't gone there –

**Mrs Linde** Yes, your father gave you the money you needed –

*Nora smiles.*

**Nora** That's what Torvald thinks – that's what they all think – but –

**Mrs Linde** But –

**Nora** Not one penny from Papa. I found the money. I did.

**Mrs Linde** You, so much money –

**Nora** Four thousand eight hundred crowns – what do you say to that?

**Mrs Linde** How, Nora? Did you win the lottery?

**Nora** The lottery is for losers – where's the skill in that?

**Mrs Linde** So where did you get it from?

*Nora hums and smiles secretively.*

You couldn't have borrowed it.

**Nora**  Couldn't I? Why not?

**Mrs Linde**  A wife cannot borrow without her husband's consent, a wife –

**Nora**  What if the wife knows something about the business – if the wife knows how to use her brains, then –

**Mrs Linde**  No, I do not understand –

**Nora**  Did I say I borrowed the money? (*She throws herself on the sofa.*) I might have had an admirer, I might have been given it, I am attractive –

**Mrs Linde**  You are mad –

**Nora**  And you're dying of curiosity, Kristine.

**Mrs Linde**  Nora, listen now – my dear, have you done something foolish –?

**Nora**  Foolish, to save your husband's life, is that foolish?

**Mrs Linde**  I think it is foolish if you did something and he did not know –

**Nora**  He was not allowed to know anything. Dear God, do you not understand? He was not allowed to know how seriously ill he was. Mortally ill – he did not know it. The doctors came to me. They told me his life was in danger. Nothing could save him unless we travelled south. Do you think I didn't try to coax him at first? I told him how lovely it would be to travel abroad like other young wives. I cried, I begged. I was on my knees. I told him to please remember my condition, to be generous and spoil me. So then I hinted he could take out a loan. Kristine, he almost lost control at that. He said I was foolish, it was his duty as a husband not to listen to my moods and my meanderings – I believe that's what he called them. Well,

17

then I thought you have to be saved, I have to save you, and I found a way out.

**Mrs Linde**  Your husband wasn't told by your father that the money didn't come from him?

**Nora**  No, never. No. Papa died. He died. I did think I'd tell him and beg him to be silent. But he was ill then. And sadly it never became necessary.

**Mrs Linde**  You've never breathed a word since to your husband?

**Nora**  For Heaven's sake, how could you think that? When it comes to money he is very strict. Torvald – Torvald is a man. He has a man's pride. He would be so ashamed and humiliated if he thought he owed me anything. It would completely upset our relationship. It would change our happy, beautiful home.

**Mrs Linde**  Will you never tell him?

*Nora half smiles and is pensive.*

**Nora**  One day I might, yes. Many years from now, when I've lost my looks a little. Don't laugh. I mean, of course, a time will come when Torvald is not as devoted to me, not quite so happy when I dance for him, and dress for him, and play with him. It might be useful then to have something up my sleeve – (*She breaks off.*) I'm talking nonsense. Nonsense. That time will never come. So, Kristine, what do you make of my secret? So, you see I am good for something but, you know, this whole affair has caused me a lot of worry. I have obligations I must fulfil on time, and they're not easy. See, there is something in the business world that's called quarterly interest and another thing called payment in instalments, and it is always terribly difficult to manage them. I had to save a little here, a little there, wherever I could. You see, I couldn't really put any of the house-keeping money aside because Torvald has to live well, and I couldn't let the children go badly dressed. Whatever I got for them I had to spend on them. They're little angels.

**Mrs Linde** So it was your needs that suffered, Nora?

**Nora** Yes, of course. It was my responsibility. When Torvald gave me money for new dresses and little things, I never spent more than half. Bought the simplest, the cheapest of materials. Thank God everything looks well on me, Torvald didn't notice. But Kristine, it was a bit hard for me. It is nice to be beautifully dressed isn't it?

**Mrs Linde** Isn't it, yes?

**Nora** I found other ways of making money as well. Last winter I was lucky enough to get a lot of copying to do. I locked myself in every evening and I wrote till late at night. I was tired. So tired. I did get such pleasure from sitting and working and earning money. It felt like . . . like being a man.

**Mrs Linde** How much have you paid off doing this?

**Nora** I can't tell you exactly. It is difficult to keep these money things in order. I do know that what I've scraped together, I've paid it all. So many times I was at my wits' end. (*She smiles.*) Sometimes I'd sit and dream there was a rich man, an old man, he fell in love with me –

**Mrs Linde** What old man, who –

**Nora** This doesn't make sense, but he'd died, they opened his will and it read, for all to see, 'To the delightful Mrs Nora Helmer, I leave all my money, paid immediately in cash –'

**Mrs Linde** Nora, who was this old man –

**Nora** Good heavens, don't you see? Nobody, he does not

exist. I just sat there and kept imagining him when I couldn't think of any way to get money. Well, he can die now. I don't need this boring old man. I don't care for him nor his will. I'm free. Free. (*She jumps up.*) Dear God, I'm free, and it is good, Kristine. Free. To be free, absolutely free. To spend time playing with the children. To have a clean, beautiful house, the way Torvald likes it. And spring will be here soon! Blue skies. Imagine it. Maybe then we can travel again. The sea, I might look on it again. Yes, yes, it is wonderful to be alive. To be happy.

*The bell is heard in the hall and Mrs Linde gets up.*

**Mrs Linde** Visitors. I'd better leave.

**Nora** Stay, please. I'm not expecting anybody. It'll be for Torvald –

*The Maid is in the doorway to the hall.*

**Maid** Excuse me, Madam, a gentleman wants to talk to the lawyer –

**Nora** The bank manager, you mean.

**Maid** Yes, the bank manager, but the doctor's still in there –

**Nora** Who is the gentleman?

*Krogstad is in the doorway to the hall.*

**Krogstad** It's myself, Madam.

*Mrs Linde frowns, starts and half turns towards the window. Nora takes a step towards him, tense, and lowers her voice.*

**Nora** You? Why? What do you want to talk to my husband about?

**Krogstad** Bank business, you might say. I've got a junior position in the Savings Bank. I now hear your husband is to be our manager.

**Nora** That's true –

**Krogstad** Yes, I merely wish to bore him with business, Madam. Nothing else.

**Nora** Please use the study door. (*She takes her leave of him indifferently as she closes the door to the hall and goes to see to the stove.*)

**Mrs Linde** Who was that, Nora? That man?

**Nora** Mr Krogstad. A lawyer.

**Mrs Linde** It was him then.

**Nora** You know that man?

**Mrs Linde** I did – years ago. I knew him. He was clerk to our local solicitor.

**Nora** Yes, that's what he was.

**Mrs Linde** He's changed an awful lot.

**Nora** A very unhappy marriage, I believe.

**Mrs Linde** Is he a widower now?

**Nora** With loads of children. There. The fire's burning. (*She closes the door to the stove and moves the rocking chair to one side.*)

**Mrs Linde** He has many business interests, they say.

**Nora** Really, is that so? Don't ask me – but business is a bore, let's not talk about it.

*Dr Rank enters from Helmer's study. He speaks in the doorway.*

**Rank** I won't disturb you, my friend. I'll pop in and see

21

your wife. (*He closes the door and remarks to Mrs Linde.*) I'm so sorry, I'm disturbing you as well.

**Nora**  You are not. Doctor Rank, Mrs Linde.

**Rank**  I see. I've heard that name often in this house. Didn't I pass you on the stairs coming in?

**Mrs Linde**  You did. I walk slowly. Stairs tire me out.

**Rank**  You're not feeling well?

**Mrs Linde**  Tired. Just tired.

**Rank**  Is that all? And you come to visit in town to get back your energy?

**Mrs Linde**  To get work, that's why I'm in town.

**Rank**  Work is now a cure for tiredness?

**Mrs Linde**  One has to live, doctor.

**Rank**  Yes, that's the general opinion.

**Nora**  Come on, Dr Rank, you must want to live as well.

**Rank**  I do, indeed. I may be a miserable fellow, but I'll go on being tormented for as long as possible. All my patients feel the same way. And people who are morally sick, they do as well. Right now Helmer is entertaining one of them –

*Mrs Linde speaks softly.*

**Mrs Linde**  What?

**Nora**  What do you mean?

**Rank**  Krogstad. A lawyer. A man you don't know. A man rotten to the core, Madam. But he too is insisting he has to live, as if it mattered so much, his life.

**Nora**  What is he talking to Torvald about?

**Rank** I do not know. Something to do with the Savings Bank.

**Nora** Does Krog – does this lawyer, Krogstad, have anything to do with the Savings Bank?

**Rank** He works there, yes, in some manner of description. (*He talks to Mrs Linde.*) Mrs Linde, I wonder if in your neck of the woods you have people who rush about sniffing out moral decay? When they find a specimen with the right smell, they stick him into some comfortable position where they can watch over him. What's to become of the morally sound? Left out in the cold, I suppose. We must heal the sick.

**Mrs Linde** Surely, it is the sick who most need healing.

*Rank shrugs his shoulders.*

**Rank** Yes, there we have it. And society turns into a hospital.

*In her own thoughts, Nora laughs to herself and claps her hands.*

You're laughing. Why? So, do you know what society is?

**Nora** What do I care about boring society? I was laughing at something quite different – something very amusing. Tell me, Dr Rank. Will everyone who works at the Savings Bank, will they all now be under Torvald?

**Rank** Is that what you find so amusing?

*Nora smiles and hums.*

**Nora** Never mind. Never you mind. (*She strolls round the floor.*) Yes, it gives me such pleasure to think that we – that Torvald has so much power over so many people. (*She takes a bag out of her pocket.*) A little macaroon, Dr Rank?

23

**Rank**  What is this? Macaroons? Aren't they illegal in this house?

**Nora**  They are, but Kristine gave me these.

**Mrs Linde**  Me – what –

**Nora**  Now, now, don't be hysterical. You didn't know that Torvald's outlawed them. No. He's afraid they will blacken my teeth. Never mind – just a little one. Yes, Dr Rank? Here you are. (*She puts a macaroon in his mouth.*) You too, Kristine. And one for me. Just a little one. Two, at the most. (*She strolls again.*) Yes, now I am a very happy woman. There is only one single thing that I really want to do, one big thing.

**Rank**  What is it?

**Nora**  Something I really want to say while Torvald's listening.

**Rank**  Why can't you say it?

**Nora**  I daren't. It's vulgar.

**Mrs Linde**  Vulgar?

**Rank**  Then don't. But say it to us – you can, surely. What do you want to say to Helmer?

**Nora**  Bloody hell.

**Rank**  Have you gone mad?

**Mrs Linde**  Nora, God help us –

**Rank**  Say it, he's here.

*Nora hides the bag of macaroons.*

**Nora**  Quiet.

*Torvald enters from his study with his coat over his arm and his hat in his hand.*

You got rid of him, did you, Torvald dear?

**Helmer** He's gone now, yes!

**Nora** Introductions. This is Kristine, who's come to town.

**Helmer** Kristine? Forgive me, I'm not sure –

**Nora** Mrs Linde. Mrs Kristine Linde, dear Torvald.

**Helmer** I see. You and my wife were friends as children?

**Mrs Linde** Yes, we knew each other long ago.

**Nora** And she has travelled a long way here just to speak to you, imagine that.

**Helmer** What is that supposed to mean?

**Mrs Linde** It's not exactly –

**Nora** You see, Kristine's very efficient at office work and she really wants to work with a clever man who will teach her much more that she already knows and direct her –

**Helmer** A sensible decision, Madam.

**Nora** So when she heard, through a telegram, that you had become manager of the bank, she raced here as quickly as she could – please, Torvald, for my sake, could you do something for Kristine? Please, please?

**Helmer** That is not impossible. I take it you are a widow?

**Mrs Linde** Yes.

**Helmer** And have some experience of office work?

**Mrs Linde** A great deal, yes.

**Helmer** Then it's quite likely I can offer you a position –

*Nora claps her hands.*

**Nora** I knew, I knew.

**Helmer** You've arrived at the right time, Mrs Linde –

**Mrs Linde** How can I thank you –

**Helmer** No need whatsoever. (*He puts on his overcoat.*) But for now you must excuse me today –

**Rank** Wait, I'll go with you. (*He fetches his fur coat from the hall and warms it by the stove.*)

**Nora** Torvald, my dear, don't stay out long.

**Helmer** An hour, no more.

**Nora** Kristine, are you leaving as well?

*Mrs Linde puts her coat on.*

**Mrs Linde** Yes, I now have to start searching for lodgings.

**Helmer** Perhaps we can walk some of the way together.

*Nora helps her.*

**Nora** It's annoying that we're so cramped for space. We just could not –

**Mrs Linde** What are you thinking of? Dear Nora, thank you for everything. Goodbye.

**Nora** For now, goodbye. But you will come back this evening, won't you? You too, Dr Rank. What do you say? Are you well enough? You will be, I know. Just wrap up well.

*During this conversation they enter the hall and the children's voices are heard outside the door.*

Here they come, here they come.

*She runs to open the door and the Nanny, Anne-Marie, enters with the children.*

Come on, come in. (*She bends down and kisses the children.*) Aren't they sweet? Aren't they angels? Do you see them, Kristine? Aren't they lovely?

**Rank** Stop talking in this draught.

**Helmer** Come along, Mrs Linde. Only a mother could bear to be here.

*Rank, Helmer and Mrs Linde go down the stairs. The Nanny enters the room with the children. Nora does so too and closes the hall door.*

**Nora** Look at those rosy red cheeks. You look so lovely I could eat you.

*The children all talk at the same time and interrupt her during the following.*

Was it great fun? Good, good. You pulled both Emmy and Bob in the sledge. Imagine that, the two of them at the same time? You're a big boy, Ivan. Anne-Marie, let me hold her a moment. My little doll, my sweet baby. (*She takes the youngest from the Nanny and dances with her.*) Yes, yes, Bob, Mummy will dance with you as well. What? Snowballs, I should have seen you throw them. Anne-Marie, I'll take off their coats myself, please don't – Yes, let me please. It is great fun. You look frozen to the bone. Go in there and drink some hot coffee – it's on the stove.

*The Nanny enters the room, stage left. Nora takes off the children's coats and throws them anywhere while she lets them chatter simultaneously.*

I see, a big bad dog chased you. Did it bite? No, it wouldn't. Doggies don't bite lovely baby dolls. Ivan, leave those parcels. What's in them? You would like to know. Well, it's something horrid. So, what will we play? What do you want to play? Hide and seek? Yes, hide and seek. Bob hides first. Me, will I hide first? All right, I'll hide.

*There is joy as Nora and the children laugh and play.
Nora finally hides under the table. The children storm
in, look, cannot find her, hear her giggling, rush to the
table, lift up the cloth and see her. There is huge excitement. There is a knock on the front door but no one
notices. The door half-opens and Krogstad appears. He
waits a little and the game continues.*

**Krogstad** I beg your pardon, Mrs Helmer –

*With a stifled scream Nora starts and turns.*

**Nora** What? What do you want?

**Krogstad** I'm sorry, the front door was open, someone
must have forgotten to shut it –

*Nora gets up.*

**Nora** My husband is not at home, Mr Krogstad.

**Krogstad** I know.

**Nora** So what do you want here then?

**Krogstad** A word with you.

**Nora** With – (*She speaks to the children who have grown
quiet.*) No, no, the strange gentleman won't hurt Mummy.
When he's gone away, we'll play again. (*She leads the children into the room, stage left, and shuts the door. She is
tense and uneasy.*) You want to talk to me?

**Krogstad** Yes, I want to talk to you.

**Nora** Why? Today isn't the first of the month –

**Krogstad** No, it's Christmas Eve. It all depends on you
whether or not you have a happy Christmas.

**Nora** What do you want? Today I can't possibly –

**Krogstad** Leave that aside. I want something else. Have

28

you a moment to spare?

**Nora** Yes, I do, I believe, but –

**Krogstad** Good. I was sitting in Olsen's cafe and saw your husband go down the street –

**Nora** Yes.

**Krogstad** With a lady.

**Nora** So?

**Krogstad** May I ask if that lady was a Mrs Linde?

**Nora** Yes.

**Krogstad** Just come to town?

**Nora** Today, yes.

**Krogstad** Isn't she a good friend of yours?

**Nora** She is yes, but why –

**Krogstad** I knew her once too.

**Nora** I know.

**Krogstad** Oh, you know about that? I thought so. All right, so I'll ask you straight out – will Mrs Linde have a position in the Savings Bank?

**Nora** Mr Krogstad, how dare you question me? You are an employee of my husband. But since you asked, I'll answer. Yes, Mrs Linde will have a position. And, Mr Krogstad, I spoke up for her. Now you know.

**Krogstad** I was right then.

*Nora paces the floor.*

**Nora** I do have a little bit of influence. Just because I am a woman, it doesn't mean – that – Mr Krogstad – you should be careful, those who are in a junior position

29

should be careful not to offend people who . . . who . . .

**Krogstad** Who have influence –

**Nora** Exactly.

*Krogstad changes his tone.*

**Krogstad** Mrs Helmer, would you please be good enough to use your influence on my behalf?

**Nora** What do you mean?

**Krogstad** Would you be kind enough to make sure that I keep my junior position in the bank?

**Nora** What are you talking about? Who's thinking of taking it from you?

**Krogstad** You don't need to pretend that you don't understand. I can well imagine why your friend isn't anxious to keep bumping into me. And I can well imagine who I've to thank for hounding me out now.

**Nora** I assure you –

**Krogstad** Yes, yes, yes – I'm getting to the point. While there is still time, I advise you to use your influence to stop this.

**Nora** Mr Krogstad, I have no influence –

**Krogstad** Have no influence? I thought you said –

**Nora** I didn't mean it in that way. Me? How can you think I have influence like that over my husband?

**Krogstad** I know your husband, we were students together. I think the bank manager is like all married men, he can be swayed.

**Nora** If you insult my husband, I'll have to ask you to leave.

**Krogstad** You are a brave lady.

**Nora** I am not afraid of you any longer. After New Year, I will soon be finished with the whole thing.

*Krogstad grows more controlled.*

**Krogstad** Madam, please listen to me. If push comes to shove, I will fight with my life to keep my little job at the bank.

**Nora** Yes, I can see that.

**Krogstad** It's not just for the money. That's the least important thing about it. There's another reason. I'll tell you. I suppose you know, everyone does, that many years ago I made a bad mistake.

**Nora** I've heard something like that, yes.

**Krogstad** It never went to court, but after that it was as though all doors were closed to me. So, I took to the business that you know about. I had to live somehow, and I honestly don't think I've been as bad as many in my trade. But now I want to give up all that. My sons are growing up. In fairness to them I need to win back what respectability I can in the town. That position in the bank was my first step on the ladder. Now your husband is going to kick me off that ladder back into the gutter.

**Nora** But honestly, Mr Krogstad, I don't have the power to help you.

**Krogstad** You don't have the inclination to help me, but I have the power to force you.

**Nora** You wouldn't tell my husband I owe you money?

**Krogstad** And if I did?

**Nora** That would be a shameful thing to do. (*She is*

*about to cry.*) I've been so proud of my secret. I couldn't bear it if he heard from you in such a clumsy, ugly way. You would put me in such an unpleasant position.

**Krogstad** Unpleasant? Is that all?

*Nora grows angry.*

**Nora** Do it then, go on, do it. See what happens then. My husband will see what a bad man you are. You certainly won't keep your position.

**Krogstad** I've just asked you if it's only domestic unpleasantness you're worried about?

**Nora** If my husband's told, he'll immediately pay what I owe you. Then we won't have anything more to do with you.

*Krogstad takes a step closer.*

**Krogstad** Mrs Helmer, listen. Is your memory failing you? Or do you really not know much about business? I will have to spell out this whole matter for you.

**Nora** What do you mean?

**Krogstad** When your husband was ill, you came to me to borrow four thousand eight hundred crowns –

**Nora** I knew no one else.

**Krogstad** I promised to get you the money.

**Nora** And you did.

**Krogstad** I promised to get you the money on certain conditions. You were so preoccupied with your husband's health, you wanted so badly to get money to travel, that I don't think you paid any attention to the details. So I should really remind you of them. I promised to get you money in a contract which I drew up.

32

**Nora** You did, and I signed.

**Krogstad** Good, but then I added another clause in which your father was to guarantee the debt. Your father was meant to sign this clause.

**Nora** Meant to? He did sign.

**Krogstad** I left the date blank. So that when your father signed the contract he could fill in the date himself. Do you remember?

**Nora** I . . . I think so –

**Krogstad** I gave you the contract to post to your father, yes?

**Nora** Yes.

**Krogstad** You must have done that straightaway, because five days – six days – later you brought it in to me with your father's signature. The amount was then paid to you.

**Nora** Yes. Well, haven't I kept up the repayments?

**Krogstad** More or less. But let's return to that date. Things were very difficult for you then, Madam?

**Nora** They were, yes.

**Krogstad** Your father was seriously ill.

**Nora** He was dying.

**Krogstad** And died shortly afterwards.

**Nora** Yes.

**Krogstad** Do you remember the day he died, the day of the month, I mean?

**Nora** Papa died on the twenty-ninth of September.

**Krogstad** That's right, I checked it. (*He takes out a piece* *of paper.*) Which leaves us with a little problem, a problem I can't solve.

**Nora** What little problem, I don't know –

**Krogstad** The problem is, Mrs Helmer, that your father signed this contract three days after his death.

**Nora** I don't understand.

**Krogstad** Your father died on the twenty-ninth of September. But look at this. Your father dated his signature the second of October. That is curious, isn't it?

*Nora is silent.*

Can you explain that to me?

*Nora remains silent.*

What is also remarkable is that the words 'the second of October' and the year are not in your father's writing, but in writing which I seem to recognize. However, that can be explained. Your father might have forgotten to date his signature and someone else might have guessed at the date before his death was known. Nothing wrong in that. It is the signature that counts. Mrs Helmer, that signature, is it genuine? It really was your father himself who signed his name here?

*After a brief silence Nora tosses her head and answers him defiantly.*

**Nora** No, he didn't. I signed Papa's name.

**Krogstad** Do you realize how dangerous this admission is?

**Nora** Why? You'll soon get your money.

**Krogstad** Can I ask you a question? Why didn't you send the contract to your father?

**Nora** I couldn't. Papa was ill. If I'd asked for his signature, I'd have had to tell him what the money was for. How could I tell him my husband's life was in such danger when he himself was so ill? I couldn't.

**Krogstad** It would have been advisable to abandon your trip abroad.

**Nora** That trip was to save my husband's life. I couldn't abandon it.

**Krogstad** Didn't it occur to you that you were defrauding me?

**Nora** I couldn't worry about that. I didn't care about you. I couldn't stand you, you were so cold, putting all of those heartless difficulties in my way when you knew my husband was dangerously ill.

**Krogstad** Mrs Helmer, I don't think you have any idea of what it is you're guilty of. But, let me tell you, my one false step that destroyed my entire reputation was nothing more or nothing worse than what you have done.

**Nora** Are you – you trying to make me believe you did something brave to save your wife's life?

**Krogstad** The law has no interest in motives.

**Nora** Then the law is very foolish.

**Krogstad** Foolish or not, if I were to present this paper to the court, you would be judged by that law.

**Nora** I don't believe that. A daughter can't protect her old, dying father? A wife can't help save her husband's life? I don't know the law very well, but I'm sure it must say somewhere that this is allowed. And if you don't know that, you, a lawyer, Mr Krogstad, you must be a very bad lawyer.

**Krogstad** Be that as it may, but I do know about business, the business we've been engaged in, and you know that. Do what you like, but I'll tell you one thing. If I'm hurled back into the gutter a second time, you will keep me company there.

*He exits through the hall. Nora, pensive for a while, tosses her head.*

**Nora** Rubbish. Trying to frighten me. I'm not that simple. (*She starts folding the children's clothes but soon stops.*) But – no, it is impossible. I did it for love.

*The children are in the doorway, stage left.*

**Children** The strange man has left now, Mummy.

**Nora** Yes, I know, yes. Now don't tell anyone about the strange man. Not even Daddy.

**Children** No, Mummy. Will you play with us again?

**Nora** No! No. Not now.

**Children** Mummy, you promised.

**Nora** Yes, but I can't now. I have so much to do. Go along, darlings, go along. (*She urges them gently out of the room and closes the door behind them. She sits down on the sofa, takes up her embroidery and sews a few stitches but soon stops.*) No. (*She throws the embroidery aside, gets up, goes to the hall door and shouts.*) Helene, let me have the tree in here. (*She goes to the table, stage left, and opens the drawer but stops again.*) No, it is all quite impossible.

*Helene enters with the Christmas tree.*

**Maid** Where will I leave it, Madam?

**Nora** The middle of the floor.

**Maid** Shall I fetch anything else?

**Nora** No, thank you, I have what I need.

*The Maid exits and Nora starts to decorate the tree.*

Candles and flowers, here and here. That creature. Nonsense, all nonsense. Nothing is wrong. Christmas tree will be lovely. Anything you want, Torvald, I will do. I will sing for you, dance –

*Helmer enters from the hall with a bundle of papers under his arm.*

Oh, you're back then?

**Helmer** Yes. Did anyone call?

**Nora** Here? No.

**Helmer** Strange. I saw Krogstad coming out the front door.

**Nora** Oh? Yes, that's true, Krogstad was here for a moment.

**Helmer** Nora, I can read you like a book. He was here asking you to put in a good word for him.

**Nora** Yes.

**Helmer** And you were told to pretend it was your idea? You also wouldn't tell me he was here. That's what he's asked you to do, yes?

**Nora** Yes, Torvald, but –

**Helmer** Nora, how could you agree to this? How, Nora? You talk to a man like that and make him promises. Then, to top it all, you tell me a lie.

**Nora** Lie?

**Helmer** Didn't you say no one had been here? (*He wags his finger.*) My singing bird must never again do that. This

37

little bird must keep its beak pure. No false notes. (*He puts his hands around her waist.*) That's so, yes? Yes, I thought so. (*He lets her go.*) So, no more about it. (*He sits down in front of the stove.*) It's so warm and cosy in here.

*He leafs through the papers. Nora busies herself with the tree. There is a short pause.*

**Nora**  Torvald.

**Helmer**  Yes.

**Nora**  I'm really looking forward to the fancy dress party the day after tomorrow – at the Sternborgs.

**Helmer**  And I'm really curious to know how you will surprise me.

**Nora**  Oh, it's really silly.

**Helmer**  Oh?

**Nora**  I can't think of anything. It's all so foolish, so dull.

**Helmer**  Is that what little Nora has decided?

*Nora is behind his chair, resting her arms on the back of it.*

**Nora**  Torvald, are you terribly busy?

**Helmer**  What?

**Nora**  What are those papers?

**Helmer**  Bank business.

**Nora**  Already?

**Helmer**  I've persuaded the retiring manager to give me authority to change staff and policy. I've to do that over Christmas. By New Year I want everything in order.

**Nora**  So that's why this poor Krogstad –

**Helmer** Hmm.

*Nora is still over the back of the chair, slowly messing up his hair.*

**Nora** Well, if you hadn't been terribly busy, I would have asked you a really, really big favour, Torvald.

**Helmer** Spell it out, what is it?

**Nora** No one has better taste than you. I so want to look good at the fancy dress party. Torvald, would you tell me what I should go as and what my costume should be?

**Helmer** Little Miss Stubbornshoes needs to be helped?

**Nora** I do, Torvald, I can't get anywhere without your help.

**Helmer** All right, I'll think about it. We'll come up with something.

**Nora** You are kind. (*She goes back to the Christmas tree. There is a pause.*) The red flowers – they look so lovely. Tell me, this Krogstad, was what he did so bad?

**Helmer** Forged signatures. Have you any idea what that means?

**Nora** Perhaps he did it out of need?

**Helmer** He could have, or because he was reckless, like so many others. I'm not heartless, I condemn no man out-right for one mistake.

**Nora** No, you wouldn't Torvald.

**Helmer** Many a man can save himself if he admits he's done wrong and takes his punishment.

**Nora** Punishment?

**Helmer** Not Krogstad though. He was cunning and

tricked his way out of it. That's when the moral rot set in.

**Nora**  Do you think that it should –

**Helmer**  Just think how a guilty man like that has to lie and cheat and deceive everyone. Imagine it: his nearest and dearest, his own wife and children, they've never seen the real man behind the mask. And the children, well that's what makes it so terrible, Nora.

**Nora**  Why?

**Helmer**  Because an atmosphere of lies like that infects and poisons the whole life of a home. In a house like that every breath the children take is filled with germs of evil.

*Nora is closer behind him.*

**Nora**  Are you sure about that?

**Helmer**  I've seen it, my darling, as a lawyer. Nearly all young criminals had lying mothers.

**Nora**  Just their mothers – why?

**Helmer**  The mother is nearly always the root of it. Every lawyer knows that only too well. Fathers do their bit as well. This Krogstad has gone home for years and poisoned his children with lies and deceit. That's why I call him an immoral man. So my sweet little Nora must promise me not to plead his case. Give me your hand. Now, now what's this? Give me your hand. Now. It's settled then. I assure you, it would have been impossible to work with him. I honestly feel sick, sick to my stomach, in the presence of such people.

*Nora withdraws her hand and goes to the other side of the Christmas tree.*

**Nora**  So hot in here – so much to do, I have –

*Helmer gets up and gathers his papers together.*

**Helmer** Yes, I'm thinking of reading some of this before dinner. I'll also think about your costume. And I might have to wrap something in gold paper on the Christmas tree. (*He puts his hand on her head.*) Bless you, my little songbird.

*He enters the study, closing the door behind him. Nora speaks quietly after a pause.*

**Nora** No, it's not possible. It isn't. It has to be impossible.

*The Nanny appears in the doorway, stage left.*

**Nanny** Your little ones ask very sweetly if they can come to Mummy.

**Nora** No, absolutely no, don't let them near me. Anne-Marie, you stay with them.

**Nanny** Very well, Madam.

*The Nanny closes the door. Nora pales from fear.*

**Nora** Poison my children – poison my home – poison them – (*There is a brief pause. She raises her head.*) It is not true. Never, never, never ever could it be true.

# Act Two

*The same living room. In the corner by the piano the Christmas tree stands, stripped of presents, dishevelled and with the remains of burned down candles. Nora's coat lies on the sofa.*

*Nora is alone, pacing the living room floor uneasily, until she finally stops by the sofa and picks up her coat. She lets go of her coat.*

**Nora** Somebody's coming. (*She turns towards the door and listens.*) Nobody – nobody. Christmas Day, no one will come today. Nor tomorrow either. But maybe – (*She opens the door and looks out.*) Nothing in the post box. Nothing. Empty. (*She walks the floor.*) This doesn't make sense. He won't do it of course. Something like this, it can't happen. It's impossible. I have little children.

*The Nanny enters from the room, stage left, with a big cardboard box.*

Thank you. Put it on the table.

*The Nanny does so.*

**Nanny** They're in an awful mess.

**Nora** I wish I could rip them into a hundred thousand pieces.

**Nanny** Dear me! They can be patched up. Have a little patience.

**Nora** Yes. I'll go out and get Mrs Linde to give me a hand.

**Nanny** Go out again? You? In this bad weather? You'll get a cold, you'll end up in bed, Mrs Helmer.

**Nora** Worse could happen. How are the children?

**Nanny** The poor darlings are playing with their Christmas presents, but –

**Nora** Are they still asking for me?

**Nanny** They're so used to having their Mummy with them.

**Nora** Yes, but Anne-Marie, from now on I can't be with them as much as I have been.

**Nanny** Little children, they get used to nearly everything.

**Nora** Do you think so? Do you think they would forget their mother if she went away for ever?

**Nanny** Dear me, for ever?

**Nora** Anne-Marie, I've often wondered, tell me, how could you bear to give your child away to be reared by strangers?

**Nanny** I had to. I was nanny to little Nora.

**Nora** Yes, but did you want to?

**Nanny** When I could get such a good position? I count myself lucky, a poor girl who'd been led astray. The man was good for nothing.

**Nora** Surely your daughter's forgotten you.

**Nanny** She has not. Twice she's written to me, when she was confirmed and when she was married.

*Nora puts her arms around Anne-Marie's neck.*

**Nora** Dear Anne-Marie, when I was a child you were a good mother.

43

**Nanny** Poor child, little Nora had no other mother but me.

**Nora** And if the children had no one else, I know that you – you – this is not making sense, I'm talking nonsense, nonsense. (*She opens the box.*) Go to them. Now I have to – Tomorrow, you'll see how beautiful I'll look.

**Nanny** Yes. Mrs Nora will be the belle of the ball.

*She exits to the room, stage left. Nora starts to unpack the box but soon throws everything down.*

**Nora** Maybe if I dared go out, but say someone came, say something happened here at home. Silly, silly. No one will come. Don't think about it. I'll brush this muff. Gorgeous gloves, gorgeous gloves. Forget about it, forget – one, two, three, four, five, six – (*She screams.*) They're coming –

*She wants to move towards the door but stands indecisively. Mrs Linde enters from the hall where she's left her outdoor clothes.*

Kristine, is that you? Is there anyone else there? I'm glad that it's you who came.

**Mrs Linde** I heard you'd come by asking for me.

**Nora** Yes, I was just passing. You must help me with something. Sit down on the sofa. Look. There is a fancy dress party at the Sternborgs tomorrow evening. Torvald wants me to go as a fisher girl from Naples and dance the tarantella. I learnt it in Capri.

**Mrs Linde** I see. You're going to give a real performance?

**Nora** Torvald wants me to. Here's the costume, look. Torvald had it made for me down there, but now it's falling to pieces and I just don't know –

**Mrs Linde** We'll soon mend it. The border is hanging down in a few places. Needle and thread? Right, we have what we need.

**Nora** This is kind of you.

*Mrs Linde sews.*

**Mrs Linde** So, tomorrow you'll be all dressed up, Nora? I'll tell you what, I'll come round for a moment and see you in your finery. But I've forgotten to say thanks for the lovely evening last night.

*Nora gets up and walks across the floor.*

**Nora** It wasn't quite as lovely here last night as it usually is. Kristine, you should have come to town a bit sooner. Yes, Torvald knows how to make a home happy and welcoming.

**Mrs Linde** And so do you. You're not your father's daughter for nothing. Tell me, is Dr Rank usually as depressed as he was yesterday?

**Nora** No. Yesterday it was very noticeable. You see, he suffers from a very serious illness. Poor man, his spine is wasting away: his father was a brute of a man. He had mistresses – things of that nature. So the son was infected from boyhood, inherited – if you follow me.

*Mrs Linde lets the sewing drop.*

**Mrs Linde** My darling Nora, how did you come to know such things?

*Nora strolls.*

**Nora** When you have given birth to three children, you get visits from . . . from ladies who possess some medical knowledge. They can tell you a thing or two.

*There is a brief pause as Mrs Linde sews.*

45

**Mrs Linde**  Does Dr Rank visit every day?

**Nora**  Every single day. He's Torvald's oldest friend – and his best friend, and he's been a good friend to me. He's like one of the family.

**Mrs Linde**  Tell me, is he sincere? Does he not rather like to flatter people?

**Nora**  Not in the least. Why do you ask that?

**Mrs Linde**  Yesterday, you introduced me to him and he assured me he had often heard my name in this house. But later I noticed that your husband had no idea who I was. How could Dr Rank –

**Nora**  Yes, that's quite right, Kristine. Torvald is so utterly and completely devoted to me. He says it, he wants me absolutely all to himself. At first he used to get quite jealous if I talked about people I loved back home. So I stopped, naturally. But I often talk to Dr Rank about such things because he likes to hear about them, you see.

**Mrs Linde**  Nora, listen, you're still a child in many ways. I'm a bit older than you and have a bit more experience. I want to tell you something. You must stop all this business with Dr Rank.

**Nora**  Stop what business?

**Mrs Linde**  The whole business. Yesterday you were talking about a rich admirer, who would get you money –

**Nora**  And who does not exist – unfortunately. What about it?

**Mrs Linde**  Is Dr Rank rich?

**Nora**  He is, yes.

**Mrs Linde**  And has no one to provide for?

**Nora** No one, but –

**Mrs Linde** He comes to this house every day?

**Nora** I've told you, yes.

**Mrs Linde** But how can such a well-bred man like that be so tactless?

**Nora** I do not understand you.

**Mrs Linde** Nora, stop pretending. Don't you realize I've guessed who loaned you the money?

**Nora** Have you gone mad? How can you imagine that? He is a friend who comes here every single day. That would be terribly embarrassing.

**Mrs Linde** So it really wasn't him?

**Nora** I assure you, no. It never entered my head for a moment – He didn't have the money then anyway. He inherited it afterwards.

**Mrs Linde** It was just as well for you, Nora my dear.

**Nora** I wouldn't have dreamed of asking Dr Rank. Mind you, I'm certain if I were to ask –

**Mrs Linde** You won't though, naturally.

**Nora** No, naturally. I don't think it would be necessary. But I'm sure if I told Dr Rank –

**Mrs Linde** Behind your husband's back?

**Nora** This other thing was behind his back too, and I have to get out of it. I have to get out of it!

**Mrs Linde** That's what I said to you yesterday, but –

*Nora paces.*

**Nora** A man knows how to manage these things much

47

better than a woman –

**Mrs Linde** Her own husband, yes.

**Nora** That's nonsense. (*She stops.*) When you pay up what you owe, you get your contract back, don't you?

**Mrs Linde** That's correct, yes.

**Nora** Then you can tear it up into a thousand pieces and burn it – that nasty, disgusting piece of paper.

*Mrs Linde puts down the sewing, gets up slowly and looks at Nora sternly.*

**Mrs Linde** Nora, you are hiding something from me.

**Nora** Can you tell?

**Mrs Linde** What is it, Nora? Something's happened to you since yesterday morning.

*Nora goes towards her.*

**Nora** Kristine. (*She listens.*) Ssh. Torvald's come home. Go in to see the children, please. Torvald hates the sight of sewing. Let Anne-Marie help you.

*Mrs Linde gathers up some items.*

**Mrs Linde** All right, but I'm not leaving until we've spoken honestly.

*Mrs Linde exits, stage left, at the same time as Helmer enters from the hall. Nora goes to meet him.*

**Nora** Torvald, I've missed you so much.

**Helmer** Was that the dressmaker?

**Nora** No. Kristine – she's helping me mend my costume. Don't worry, I'll look fine.

**Helmer** Yes, that was a rather clever idea of mine.

**Nora** Wonderful. But aren't I good to give in to you?

*Helmer lifts her chin.*

**Helmer** Good – because you give in to your husband? You funny little thing. I know you didn't mean it like that. Go on, I won't trouble you. I imagine you want to try it on.

**Nora** And I imagine you need to work?

**Helmer** Yes. (*He shows her a bundle of papers.*) Look, I've been to the bank – (*He is about to enter his study.*)

**Nora** Torvald.

*He stops.*

**Helmer** Yes?

**Nora** Say your little bird were to ask you for something very prettily –

**Helmer** What?

**Nora** Would you do it?

**Helmer** I would have to know what it is first.

**Nora** Your squirrel will run around and play if you're kind and do what I want.

**Helmer** Out with it.

**Nora** Your skylark would sing in all the rooms –

**Helmer** So? My skylark does that anyway.

**Nora** I'd work magic in the moonlight and dance for you, Torvald.

**Helmer** Nora, surely this hasn't anything to do with what you mentioned this morning?

*Nora moves closer.*

**Nora** Yes. I beg you with all my heart, Torvald.

**Helmer** You really have the nerve to bring this up again?

**Nora** Yes, you must do as I ask, please, you must let Krogstad keep his job at the bank.

**Helmer** I've decided to give his job to Mrs Linde, dear Nora.

**Nora** That is very, very kind of you. But couldn't you get rid of another clerk instead of Krogstad?

**Helmer** I do not believe how stubborn you are. Just because you've made him a foolish promise, I have to –

**Nora** That's not the reason, Torvald. I'm only thinking about you. The man writes in the most dreadful news-papers. You've said that yourself. He can do you untold harm. I'm frightened to death of him.

**Helmer** Now I understand. You're frightened by old memories.

**Nora** What do you mean?

**Helmer** Your father – that's who you're thinking about.

**Nora** I am, yes. I am. People wrote such wicked things about Papa in the papers. Remember that. They slandered him so viciously. I'm sure he would have been dismissed if they hadn't sent you to look into it. You were so kind, you helped him so much.

**Helmer** My little Nora, there is a very big difference between your father and myself. As a civil servant your father's reputation was not beyond reproach. Mine is. And I hope it will remain so, for as long as I hold my position.

**Nora** But you never know what harm people can do. We could be so comfortable now, so content, so happy in our peaceful home – you and me and the children, Torvald. That is why I really do beg you –

**Helmer** The more you plead for him, the more impossible it is for me to keep him. Everyone in the bank knows I'm going to get rid of Krogstad. If word got about that the bank manager let his wife change his mind –

**Nora** So, what then?

**Helmer** I'll tell you what then. If little Miss Stubborn-shoes gets her way, I'd be made a laughing stock before the entire staff. People would start to think I didn't have a mind of my own. Believe you me, I'd soon have to face the consequences. Anyway, there is another reason why it is quite impossible for Krogstad to stay in the bank while I am manager.

**Nora** What?

**Helmer** If I were pushed to it, I could overlook his moral failings –

**Nora** Yes, you could, Torvald.

**Helmer** I'm told he could be quite useful. But we've known each other from being students together. It's one of those ill-judged friendships that you so often come to regret in later life. I'm telling you the truth now. We call each other by our first names. But this man has no tact, he continues to do so even when other people are present. In fact, he thinks he has a right to be very familiar with me. He keeps interrupting all the time with 'Torvald this', 'Torvald that'. It's so embarrassing. He would make my position at the bank absolutely impossible.

**Nora** You can't mean this, Torvald.

**Helmer** Why can't I?

**Nora** Because it's such a petty reason.

51

**Helmer** Petty? What are you saying? You think I'm petty?

**Nora** I don't, Torvald. Darling, this is precisely why –

**Helmer** Never mind that. You describe my reasons as petty, that means I am petty too. Petty. Never – I – I can put an end to all of this. (*He goes to the hall door and shouts.*) Helene.

**Nora** What are you going to do?

*Helmer looks through his papers.*

**Helmer** To settle this.

*The Maid enters.*

This letter, take it. Go downstairs, find a messenger, and tell him to deliver it. Do it quickly. The address is on the envelope. Here's some money.

**Maid** Yes, sir.

*The Maid leaves with the letter. Helmer tidies up his papers.*

**Helmer** There you have it, little Miss Stubbornshoes.

*Nora speaks breathlessly.*

**Nora** Torvald – what was that letter?

**Helmer** Krogstad's dismissal.

**Nora** Torvald, get it back. There's still time. Get it back, Torvald. For my sake, do it. Your own sake, the children. Do it, Torvald. You don't know what this could do to us all.

**Helmer** It's too late.

**Nora** Too late, yes.

**Helmer** Dear Nora, I can forgive you because you are

frightened, though actually it's an insult. Yes it is. Don't you see it's insulting to think I would be frightened because some failed, depraved hack wants revenge against me? Well, maybe insult is too strong, but I forgive you anyway, because this shows me, this proves to me, how beautifully and how bravely you love me. (*He takes her in his arms.*) My own darling Nora, that's how it should be. Whatever happens, when a real crisis comes, you'll see, I have strength and courage for both of us. You'll see that I'm man enough to deal with everything myself.

*Nora is terrified.*

**Nora** What do you mean by that?

**Helmer** Everything I say.

*Nora grows composed.*

**Nora** You will never, ever have to do that.

**Helmer** Good. Then we'll share everything, Nora – as man and wife. As it should be. (*He caresses her.*) Happy now? There, there, there, don't show me those frightened eyes, my dove. It's all in your imagination. Now you ought to practise the tarantella, with your tambourine. I'll go to the study and close the door so I won't hear anything. Make as much noise as you like. (*He turns around in the doorway.*) When Rank comes, tell him where I am.

*He nods to her, goes with his papers to his study and closes the door. Nora stands rooted to the floor, despairing with anxiety, and whispers.*

**Nora** He is capable of doing it. He will do it. He will do it, no matter what. No, never, never ever. Never, ever. Save me – a way out –

*The bell rings in the hall.*

53

Anything rather than that – anything, no matter what it may be.

*She wipes her face, pulls herself together and goes to open the door to the hall. Dr Rank stands outside and is hanging up his fur coat. During their conversation it begins to grow dark.*

**Nora** Dr Rank, it's you. Don't go into Torvald yet, I believe he's busy.

**Rank** And you?

*Rank enters the room and Nora closes the door behind him.*

**Nora** Me? You know I always have time to spare for you.

**Rank** Thank you. I'll enjoy that for as long as I can.

**Nora** As long as you can? What do you mean?

**Rank** Does that frighten you?

**Nora** It's a curious expression. What could happen?

**Rank** I've long been prepared for what could happen. I simply didn't think it would happen so soon.

*Nora clasps his arms.*

**Nora** What have you been told? Tell me, Dr Rank.

*Rank sits down by the stove.*

**Rank** I'm going downhill, and nothing's to be done.

*Nora breathes a sigh of relief.*

**Nora** So it's you –

**Rank** Who else? It's pointless lying to myself. Physician, heal thyself, but I am beyond healing. These past few days I've taken stock of the state I'm in. Bankrupt. Within a

54

month I may be rotting in the churchyard.

**Nora** That's a hideous thing to say.

**Rank** It is hideous, and the worst thing is it will grow more and more hideous. I've a few more tests to do. When I've done that, I should know when the disintegration begins. There is something I want to tell you. Helmer is so fastidious, he cannot face up to anything ugly. I don't want him in my sick room –

**Nora** Dr Rank, please –

**Rank** I don't want him there. Absolutely not. I'll lock my door to him as soon as I know the very worst. When I send my visiting card to you, with a black cross on it, you'll know then that my terrible death has come calling.

**Nora** You're very unreasonable today and I so wanted you to be in a good mood.

**Rank** Staring death in the face? And all to pay for someone else's sins. Where's the justice in that? There is a law of retribution. It's merciless. And it touches someone in every family –

*Nora covers her ears.*

**Nora** That is nonsense. Happy – be happy.

**Rank** Yes, laugh at it – that's all we can do. My poor spine is innocent, but my father was a soldier and he enjoyed his life, so I must suffer.

*Nora is at the table, stage left.*

**Nora** He was rather too fond of asparagus and pâté de foie gras. Wasn't that so?

**Rank** He was, and truffles. Devoured them.

**Nora** Truffles, yes. Oysters as well?

55

**Rank** Yes, oysters. Quite so, oysters.

**Nora** Port and champagne. Such delectable things. It's unfortunate that such delicious things affect the spine.

**Rank** Especially the unhappy spine that's had no pleasure from them at all.

**Nora** Yes, that is most unfortunate.

*Rank looks at her searchingly.*

**Rank** Yes.

*A short pause.*

**Nora** Why did you smile?

**Rank** No, you laughed.

**Nora** No, Dr Rank, you smiled.

*Rank gets up.*

**Rank** You're capable of much more mischief than I'd ever imagined.

**Nora** I am in the mood for madness today.

**Rank** So it appears.

*Nora places both her hands on his shoulders.*

**Nora** My dear Dr Rank, you're not going to die on Torvald and me.

**Rank** You'll soon get over the loss. Those out of sight are soon out of mind.

*Nora looks at him fearfully.*

**Nora** You think so?

**Rank** New friends appear and then –

**Nora** What new friends?

**Rank** When I am gone, you and Helmer will find new friends. I believe that's started already. What was this Mrs Linde doing here last night?

**Nora** You can't be jealous of poor Kristine?

**Rank** I am, yes. She will succeed me in this house. When I'm dead and buried perhaps that woman will –

**Nora** Ssh. Not so loud. She's in there.

**Rank** Today already? You see.

**Nora** Only mending my costume. Good heavens, you are being unreasonable. (*She sits down on the sofa.*) Dr Rank, please be nice. You'll see tomorrow how beautifully I can dance. You must imagine I dance only for you – and for Torvald as well – that goes without saying. (*She takes various items from the box.*) Dr Rank, sit down. I've something to show you. (*She sits down.*)

**Rank** What is it?

**Nora** Look. See.

**Rank** Silk stockings.

**Nora** The colour of flesh. Lovely, aren't they? Yes, it's so dark in here, but tomorrow – No, no, no. Only the foot. Well, I'll allow you to look a little higher.

**Rank** Well.

**Nora** You look so disapproving – why? Do you think they may not fit?

**Rank** I do not know, I don't possess that information.

*Nora looks at him for a moment.*

**Nora** Shame, shame. (*She hits him lightly on the ear with the stockings.*) That will teach you. (*She packs them away again.*)

**Rank** What other beauties shall I get to see?

**Nora** You won't get to see anything more because you are a bold boy. (*She hums a little and searches among the items. There is a short pause.*)

**Rank** When we sit like this, like intimates, I cannot understand, cannot comprehend what would have become of me if I had never entered this house.

*Nora smiles.*

**Nora** Yes, I do think you feel at home with us.

*Rank looks away and speaks more quietly.*

**Rank** And to leave it all, to have to leave –

**Nora** Nonsense, you won't leave.

*Rank continues in the same tone.*

**Rank** To leave no token of thanks behind. To be barely missed. Nothing left but empty space, which anyone can fill.

**Nora** If I were to ask you – nothing.

**Rank** What?

**Nora** For a great proof of your friendship –

**Rank** Yes, what?

**Nora** I mean – an extraordinary favour –

**Rank** Would you really make me so happy?

**Nora** You don't even know what it is.

**Rank** Then ask it.

**Nora** I can't, no Dr Rank. It's too much – far too much. I need advice and help, I need a favour –

**Rank** All you ask for. I do not understand what you mean, I can't. But ask. Don't you trust me?

**Nora** Yes, more than anyone else. You know you are my most loyal, most faithful friend. So I will tell you. Dr Rank, this is something you must help me stop happening. You know how much Torvald loves me – how unbelievably much he loves me. There isn't a moment when he wouldn't give his life for me.

*Rank leans towards her.*

**Rank** Nora, do you think he is the only one –

*Nora jolts lightly.*

**Nora** Who –

**Rank** Who would gladly give his life for you?

*Nora answers sadly.*

**Nora** So.

**Rank** I swore to myself that you would know this before I'd go away. I will never find a better opportunity. Yes, now you know, Nora. And now you always know that you can trust me as you can trust no one else.

*Nora rises and speaks calmly and quietly.*

**Nora** Let me pass.

*Rank remains seated but makes room for her.*

**Rank** Nora –

*Nora stands in the door to the hall.*

**Nora** Bring in the lamp, Helene. (*She goes to the stove.*) That was extremely wicked of you, Dr Rank.

*Rank gets up.*

**Rank** Wicked? To have loved you as deeply as any other –

**Nora** Wicked that you should go and tell me. It was not necessary –

**Rank** What do you mean? Did you know –

*The Maid enters with the lamp, puts it on the table and exits.*

I'm asking you, Nora, Mrs Helmer, did you know something?

**Nora** Did I know, did I not know – what of it? I can't tell you. Dr Rank, how could you be so insensitive? When everything was going so well.

**Rank** At least you know now that I'm absolutely yours, body and soul. And will you now ask?

*Nora looks at him.*

**Nora** After this?

**Rank** I'm begging you, let me know what it is.

**Nora** No, not now.

**Rank** Don't punish me like this. I'll do what is humanly possible, if you'll let me.

**Nora** What can you do for me now? Nothing. Anyway, I don't need help. It's all in my imagination. All in my imagination. Naturally. (*She sits in the rocking chair, looks at him and smiles.*) Well, you really are some gentleman, Dr Rank. Should you not be ashamed of yourself, now the lamp has come in?

**Rank** I'm not, no. Should I leave – for good?

**Nora** You mustn't do that, no. You must of course come here as always. You know very well that Torvald can't do without you.

**Rank**  Can you?

**Nora**  I do think it is such enormous fun when you're here.

**Rank**  That's exactly what I misinterpreted. You're a mystery to me. Often it seems to me you like my company almost as much as Helmer's.

**Nora**  You see, there are people one loves and then there are others whose company one almost prefers.

**Rank**  There is something in that.

**Nora**  When I lived at home, I loved Papa more than anyone else in the world, but I always thought it great fun to hide down with the maids. They didn't tell me what I ought to do and they had such a good time together.

**Rank**  And I have now taken the place of the maids.

*Nora jumps up and goes to him.*

**Nora**  Dear kind Dr Rank, that was not what I meant at all. But you can imagine being with Torvald is a little bit like being with Papa.

*The Maid enters from the hall.*

**Maid**  Madam.

*The Maid whispers and hands Nora a visiting card. Nora glances at the card.*

**Nora**  Oh! (*She puts it in her pocket.*)

**Rank**  Is something wrong?

**Nora**  Nothing whatsoever. Something – something about my new costume –

**Rank**  Your costume's over there.

**Nora**  It is, yes. This is another I've ordered. Torvald mustn't know –

**Rank**  The great secret is revealed.

**Nora**  Yes. Go in to him, he's in the study. Keep him busy for a while –

**Rank**  Worry not. He won't escape from me.

*He enters Helmer's study. Nora addresses the Maid.*

**Nora**  Is he waiting in the kitchen?

**Maid**  Yes, he came up the back way.

**Nora**  Did you not tell him I had a visitor?

**Maid**  I did, but it made no difference.

**Nora**  He won't leave?

**Maid**  Not until he's spoken to you, Madam.

**Nora**  Then show him in. Do it quietly. Helene, don't breathe a word of this. He's bringing a surprise for my husband.

**Maid**  I understand, yes. (*She exits.*)

**Nora**  So it's happening, this terrible thing. It's going to happen. No, it can't happen. It shall not happen.

*She goes and locks the door to Helmer's study. The Maid opens the door to Krogstad and closes it after him. He is dressed in a fur coat for travelling, a fur hat and galoshes. Nora turns towards him.*

Keep your voice down, my husband's at home.

**Krogstad**  I don't care.

**Nora**  What do you want from me?

**Krogstad**  I want an explanation.

**Nora**  Hurry up then. What is it?

**Krogstad**  I suppose you know I've been dismissed.

**Nora**  Mr Krogstad, I could not stop that. I fought for you as well as I could. It was useless.

**Krogstad**  Your husband can't love you very much, can he? He knows I can expose you to the world and yet he dares to dismiss me.

**Nora**  How can you imagine he knows anything –

**Krogstad**  Ah, I didn't think so. No. Old Torvald Helmer wouldn't be man enough.

**Nora**  Mr Krogstad, show some respect to my husband, please.

**Krogstad**  But of course, all the respect he deserves. But since you seem so anxious to keep this matter to yourself, I presume you know a little more than yesterday what precisely you have done?

**Nora**  More than you could ever teach me.

**Krogstad**  Yes, a bad lawyer like myself –

**Nora**  What is it you want from me?

**Krogstad**  Just to see how you were, Mrs Helmer. I've been thinking about you all day. Even money-lenders, hacks, well, a man like me, can have a little of what you call feeling, you know.

**Nora**  Show it then. My little children, think of them.

**Krogstad**  Have you thought of mine? Has your husband? Still, let that pass. I just want to tell you not to take this business too seriously. I am not going to make any accusation for the time being.

**Nora**  No, no. I know you wouldn't do anything really.

**Krogstad**  This can all be dealt with quite amicably.

There's no reason why anyone else should know anything about it. It will be just between ourselves, the three of us.

**Nora**  My husband must never know anything about this.

**Krogstad**  How will you stop him? Unless, of course, you can pay off the rest of the debt.

**Nora**  Not at the moment, no.

**Krogstad**  Well, perhaps you have found a way of getting the money in the next few days, yes?

**Nora**  No way that I'd want to use.

**Krogstad**  It would be pointless anyway. If you stood here with your fists full of bank notes, you wouldn't get your contract back from me.

**Nora**  Tell me how you want to use it.

**Krogstad**  I just want to keep it – have it in my possession. No one else will know anything about it. So if all this has made you think of doing something desperate –

**Nora**  It has.

**Krogstad**  If you were thinking of running away –

**Nora**  I am.

**Krogstad**  Or something worse –

**Nora**  How do you know?

**Krogstad**  Put that thought out of your mind.

**Nora**  How do you know I was thinking about that?

**Krogstad**  Most of us think of that first. I thought of it too. But I didn't have the courage –

**Nora**  Neither do I –

*Krogstad is relieved.*

64

**Krogstad** That's it, isn't it. You haven't the courage either, do you?

**Nora** No, I don't. I don't.

**Krogstad** Besides, it would be very foolish. Once the first domestic storm is over – I have a letter here in my pocket for your husband –

**Nora** Telling him everything?

**Krogstad** As delicately as possible.

*Nora speaks quickly.*

**Nora** He mustn't get that letter. Tear it up. I'll find the money.

**Krogstad** Mrs Helmer, I beg your pardon, haven't I just explained –

**Nora** I don't mean the money I owe you. Just tell me how much you want from my husband and I'll get it.

**Krogstad** I don't want money from your husband.

**Nora** What do you want?

**Krogstad** I'll tell you. I want to get back on my feet, Mrs Helmer. I want to get on and that's where your husband is going to help me. For the past eighteen months I've not had a hand in anything dishonourable. All that time I've lived in extreme hardship. I was prepared to work my way up step by step. Now I've been thrown down again I won't be satisfied with being reinstated as a favour. I want to get on, I tell you. I want to get back into that bank again in a higher position. Your husband will make a place for me.

**Nora** He will never do that.

**Krogstad** He will. I know him. And he won't dare say a

65

word. Once I'm in there, with him, wait and see. I give it a year and I'll be the bank manager's right-hand man. Nils Krogstad will run the Savings Bank, *not* Torvald Helmer.

**Nora**  Not in your lifetime, or mine.

**Krogstad**  So you may do something –

**Nora**  I have the courage now.

**Krogstad**  You can't frighten me. A fine, spoilt lady –

**Nora**  You'll see. You'll see.

**Krogstad**  Under the ice, perhaps? Sinking into the black, cold water? And then, in the spring, floating to the surface, ugly, unrecognizable, with your hair fallen out.

**Nora**  You can't frighten me.

**Krogstad**  Nor you me. No fear whatsoever. Mrs Helmer, people don't do things like that. Besides, what would be the point? I have him buried in my pocket.

**Nora**  But afterwards – when I am gone –

**Krogstad**  Don't forget that your reputation would still be in my hands.

*Nora stands and looks at him, speechless.*

I've prepared you now. Don't do anything foolish. I shall expect to hear from Helmer as soon as he gets my letter. And remember, it's him, your husband, who's forced me to do this kind of thing again. I will never forgive him for that. Goodbye, Mrs Helmer.

*He exits through the hall. Nora goes towards the hall door, opens it a little and listens.*

**Nora**  He's not going to give him the letter. No, he's not. Not possible.

*A letter falls into the post box. We hear Krogstad's foot-steps which gradually diminish as he goes down the stairs. Nora gives a stifled cry, runs across the floor to the sofa table. There is a short pause.*

The post box. The letter's there. Torvald, Torvald – we are lost.

*Mrs Linde enters with the costume.*

**Mrs Linde** I've mended everything. Do you want to try it on –

*Nora speaks hoarsely, in a stifled way.*

**Nora** Kristine, come here.

*Mrs Linde throws the clothes on the sofa.*

**Mrs Linde** What's wrong? Why are you so upset?

**Nora** Come here. Do you see that letter? Look – through the glass – in the post box.

**Mrs Linde** Yes, I can see it.

**Nora** A letter from Krogstad –

**Mrs Linde** Nora – it was Krogstad who lent you the money.

**Nora** Yes. Now Torvald will know everything.

**Mrs Linde** Nora, believe me, this is the best thing for you both.

**Nora** You don't understand. I forged a signature –

**Mrs Linde** Oh my God –

**Nora** I want to tell you, Kristine, so you will be my witness.

**Mrs Linde** Witness to what?

**Nora** If I go out of my mind – which may happen –

**Mrs Linde**  Nora –

**Nora**  Or if anything were to happen to me – if I could not stay here any longer –

**Mrs Linde**  Nora, Nora, you are not out of your mind –

**Nora**  If someone were to take it all on himself, all the blame –

**Mrs Linde**  Yes, but how can you think –

**Nora**  You will be my witness that it's not true, Kristine. I am not mad, I am not. I know exactly what I'm saying. And, I tell you, no one else knew about it, I did it all alone. Remember that.

**Mrs Linde**  I will. But I don't understand this.

**Nora**  How could you understand? Something glorious is going to happen.

**Mrs Linde**  Something glorious?

**Nora**  Glorious, yes. But it's frightening, Kristine. It can't happen, not for anything in the world.

**Mrs Linde**  I'm going to talk to Krogstad.

**Nora**  Don't. He'll harm you.

**Mrs Linde**  He would have done anything for me once.

**Nora**  Him?

**Mrs Linde**  Where does he live?

**Nora**  How would I – yes. (*She reaches in her pocket.*) His card. But the letter, the letter –

*In his study, Helmer knocks on the door.*

**Helmer**  Nora.

*Nora screams with fear.*

68

**Nora**  What? What do you want?

**Helmer**  It's all right. Don't be so frightened. We won't barge in. You've locked the door. Are you trying on your costume?

**Nora**  Yes, that's right, my costume – I'm trying it on. I'll look so beautiful, Torvald.

*Mrs Linde has read the card.*

**Mrs Linde**  He lives just around the corner.

**Nora**  There's no point. We're lost. The letter is in the box.

**Mrs Linde**  Does your husband have the key?

**Nora**  Yes, always.

**Mrs Linde**  Krogstad must ask for his letter back, he must think of an excuse –

**Nora**  But now is just the time when Torvald –

**Mrs Linde**  Delay him. Do something. Go into him. I'll be back as soon as I can.

*She exits through the hall door. Nora goes to Helmer's room, opens it and looks inside.*

**Nora**  Torvald?

*Helmer speaks from the study.*

**Helmer**  So, I'm allowed back into my own drawing room, am I? Come on, Rank, let's take a look – (*He is in the doorway.*) What's going on?

**Nora**  What, my darling?

**Helmer**  Rank had me all prepared for a great costume change.

*Rank is in the doorway.*

**Rank** That's what I understood. But it seems I was wrong.

**Nora** Until tomorrow no one will see me in my finery.

**Helmer** Nora dear, you look worn out. Have you been practising too much?

**Nora** No, I've not practised at all.

**Helmer** You will have to –

**Nora** I most definitely will have to, yes, Torvald. But I'm useless without your help. I've forgotten everything, honestly.

**Helmer** We'll soon polish it up again.

**Nora** Yes, look after me, Torvald, please. Promise me that, please? I'm so nervous. It's such a big party. You must give up your whole evening to me. Not a word about business. No pen in your hand. You will, won't you, Torvald?

**Helmer** Promise. Tonight I will be wholly at your service. You helpless little thing. But first I must – (*He goes towards the hall door.*)

**Nora** What do you want out there?

**Helmer** To see if any letters have been delivered.

**Nora** No don't, Torvald. No.

**Helmer** What is it now?

**Nora** I beg you, Torvald. There's nothing there.

**Helmer** Let me see anyway.

*He makes to go. Nora, by the piano, dances the first bars of the tarantella. By the door, Helmer stops.*

Aha.

**Nora**  I can't dance tomorrow if I don't practise the steps for you.

*Helmer goes to her.*

**Helmer**  Are you really so nervous, darling?

**Nora**  I am. I am so terribly nervous. Let me rehearse now. There's still time before dinner. Torvald, please sit down and play for me. Teach me, correct me the way you usually do.

**Helmer**  With pleasure, if you want that, with great pleasure.

*He arranges himself at the piano. Nora takes the tambourine and a long, multi-coloured shawl from the box. She quickly throws it about herself and springs onto the floor and shouts.*

**Nora**  Play for me – play – I want to dance.

*He plays and she dances. Rank stands behind Helmer at the piano and watches. Helmer continues playing.*

**Helmer**  Slow down – slow down.

**Nora**  I can't dance any other way.

**Helmer**  Nora, it's too violent.

**Nora**  It has to be just like this.

*Helmer stops playing.*

**Helmer**  No, no, this is no good at all.

*Nora laughs and swings the tambourine.*

**Nora**  What did I tell you?

**Rank**  Let me play for her.

*Helmer gets up.*

**Helmer** Do, please. Then I can teach her better.

*Rank sits down at the piano and plays. Nora dances more and more wildly. Helmer positions himself by the stove. During the dance Helmer keeps addressing corrective comments to Nora. She does not appear to hear them. She does not notice her hair come loose and fall over her shoulders. She keeps dancing. Mrs Linde enters and stands as if glued to the floor.*

**Mrs Linde** My.

*Nora calls out, still dancing.*

**Nora** Kristine, look – such fun.

**Helmer** Nora, my love, you dance as if your life depends on it.

**Nora** It does.

**Helmer** Rank, stop it – this is utter insanity. I'm telling you – stop.

*Rank stops playing and Nora stops suddenly. Helmer goes to her.*

I cannot believe this – I really cannot. You've forgotten everything I taught you.

*Nora throws down the tambourine.*

**Nora** See – see.

**Helmer** I see you certainly need instruction.

**Nora** Yes, you see how much I need you. You must teach me right up to the last step. Do you promise me that, Torvald?

**Helmer** You can rely on it.

72

**Nora** You must think of no one but me, not today, not tomorrow. No letters – don't even open the post box –

**Helmer** Still frightened of that person?

**Nora** Yes, that as well, yes.

**Helmer** Nora, a letter's already come from him, I can tell.

**Nora** I don't know. There might be. But don't read anything now. Nothing ugly should come between us until all this is finished.

*Rank speaks quietly to Helmer.*

**Rank** It might be wise not to cross her.

*Helmer embraces her.*

**Helmer** The child commands and I'll obey. But tomorrow evening, when you've danced –

**Nora** You're free then.

*The Maid is at the door, stage right.*

**Maid** Dinner is served, Madam.

**Nora** Champagne, we'll drink champagne.

**Maid** Very well, Madam. (*She exits.*)

**Helmer** I see, I see – a big party now?

**Nora** Let's drink champagne till dawn. (*She shouts.*) And macaroons, Helene, a few – lots – just this once.

*Helmer takes her hands.*

**Helmer** Come on now, this excitement has upset you. Please, be my skylark again, please.

**Nora** I will be. But just for now, go in there. You too, Dr Rank. Kristine, you must help me tie up my hair.

73

*Rank is subdued as they leave.*

**Rank** What is this – I mean, she's not expecting is she?

**Helmer** Most certainly not, my friend. I told you she was like a child, fretting about this.

*They exit, stage right.*

**Nora** Well?

**Mrs Linde** Gone to the country.

**Nora** Your face said it all.

**Mrs Linde** He'll be back tomorrow evening. I left him a note.

**Nora** You shouldn't have. Let it all happen. It's thrilling, isn't it, waiting for something glorious to happen.

**Mrs Linde** What are you waiting for?

**Nora** You wouldn't understand. Go in and join them. I'll be in in a minute.

*Mrs Linde goes into the dining room. Nora stands a while, collects herself, then looks at her watch.*

Five o'clock. Midnight is seven hours away. Twenty-four hours until the next midnight. The tarantella will have passed. Twenty-four and seven. Thirty-one hours to live.

*Helmer is at the door, stage right.*

**Helmer** What's keeping my little skylark?

*Nora goes towards him with outstretched arms.*

**Nora** Your skylark is flying to you.

# Act Three

*The same room. The sofa table has been moved to the middle of the floor with chairs around it. A lamp burns on the table. The door to the hall is open. Dance music can be heard from the floor above.*

*Mrs Linde sits by the table and tries to read, leafing through a book, unable to concentrate. A few times she listens intently towards the hall door. She looks at her watch.*

**Mrs Linde**  No sign of him. There's not much time left. I hope he hasn't – (*She listens again.*) He's here. (*She goes to the hall and opens the door cautiously. Quiet steps can be heard on the stairs and she whispers.*) Come in, no one's here.

*Krogstad is in the doorway.*

**Krogstad**  I found a note from you at home. What is this about?

**Mrs Linde**  I have to speak to you.

**Krogstad**  Oh, have you? Does it have to be in this house?

**Mrs Linde**  It is not possible at my lodgings. My room does not have its own entrance. We're on our own. Come in. The maid's asleep and the Helmers are upstairs at a dance.

*Krogstad enters the room.*

**Krogstad**  I see. So, the Helmers dance tonight? They're dancing?

**Mrs Linde**  Why shouldn't they dance?

**Krogstad**  Absolutely. Why shouldn't they dance?

**Mrs Linde**  It's time for us to talk.

**Krogstad**  Do we have anything more to talk about?

**Mrs Linde**  We have a great deal to talk about.

**Krogstad**  I shouldn't have thought so.

**Mrs Linde**  You don't, because you have never really understood me.

**Krogstad**  Was there anything to understand, except what was clear to everybody? A heartless woman dumps a man when she's offered a better deal.

**Mrs Linde**  Do you think I have no heart? Do you think I left you with an easy heart?

**Krogstad**  Didn't you?

**Mrs Linde**  Did you really think that?

**Krogstad**  Then why did you write to me the way you did?

**Mrs Linde**  What else could I do? I had to leave you, and so I had to destroy everything you felt for me.

*Krogstad clenches his fist.*

**Krogstad**  So that's what you did – and all this you did for money.

**Mrs Linde**  You mustn't forget I had a helpless mother and two small brothers. We couldn't wait for you, Nils. Your prospects were so remote then.

**Krogstad**  Even so. But you did not have the right to throw me aside like that for someone else.

76

**Mrs Linde** I really don't know. I've questioned myself many times if I had that right.

*Krogstad speaks more quietly.*

**Krogstad** When I lost you, I lost my bearings – it was as if the solid ground had given way under my feet. Look at me. Now I'm wrecked, the ship's gone and I'm a man clinging to wreckage.

**Mrs Linde** Help might be looking you in the face.

**Krogstad** It was looking me in the face, but you've come and got in the way.

**Mrs Linde** I didn't know that. I didn't know until today that I was to replace you at the bank.

**Krogstad** I believe you if you say so. But now you do know it, are you going to resign?

**Mrs Linde** No. Because it would not help you in the slightest if I did.

**Krogstad** Help? Help? Yes. Well, I would have done it.

**Mrs Linde** I've learned to be practical. Life and hard bitter necessity have taught me that.

**Krogstad** And life has taught me not to believe in fine words.

**Mrs Linde** Then life has taught you something useful. But do you believe in doing something?

**Krogstad** What do you mean by that?

**Mrs Linde** You said you were like a shipwrecked man clinging to wreckage.

**Krogstad** I had good reason to say that.

**Mrs Linde** Well I'm like a shipwrecked woman, clinging

to the wreckage as well. I've no one to care about, no one to care for.

**Krogstad** You yourself chose that.

**Mrs Linde** There was no other choice then.

**Krogstad** So, what about it?

**Mrs Linde** Nils, suppose these two shipwrecked people could reach each other?

**Krogstad** What are you saying?

**Mrs Linde** It's better that two people cling to the wreckage rather than one person on his own.

**Krogstad** Kristine.

**Mrs Linde** Why do you think I've come to this town?

**Krogstad** Were you really thinking about me?

**Mrs Linde** If I'm to survive in this life, I have to work. All my life, as long as I remember, I have worked. It's been my one and only great joy. But now I am alone – in the world. I am alone, and I am empty. And there is no joy in working for yourself alone. Give me something, Nils. Give me someone to work for.

**Krogstad** I don't believe this. This is a woman's hysterical, high-minded obsession with sacrificing herself –

**Mrs Linde** Have you ever known me to be hysterical?

**Krogstad** Could you really do this? Could you? Tell me. Do you know all about my past life?

**Mrs Linde** Yes.

**Krogstad** And you know my reputation here?

**Mrs Linde** You've just said, you've just implied, with me you could have been someone else.

78

**Krogstad** I'm certain of it.

**Mrs Linde** Surely it could still happen?

**Krogstad** Kristine, do you know what you're saying? You do, yes. I can see it. Do you really have the courage?

**Mrs Linde** I need to care for someone, and your children need a mother. You and I need each other. Nils, I believe in you. I believe in what you really are. With you, I'd dare to do anything.

*He clasps her hands.*

**Krogstad** Thank you . . . thank you . . . Kristine . . . I will rise again, I know how to . . . I will make other people see me in the same way . . . but I forgot –

*She listens.*

**Mrs Linde** Ssh. The tarantella. Move, go on.

**Krogstad** Why? What is it?

**Mrs Linde** The dance upstairs, can you hear it? They'll be coming back when it's over.

**Krogstad** Right, I must go. But this is all for nothing. You don't know what I've done to the Helmers, do you?

**Mrs Linde** I do know.

**Krogstad** Even so, you've still the courage –

**Mrs Linde** I also know what a man like you can do in despair.

**Krogstad** If only I could stop what I've done –

**Mrs Linde** You can. Your letter is still in the box.

**Krogstad** Are you certain?

**Mrs Linde** Certain, but –

*He looks at her searchingly.*

**Krogstad** What is this? You'd do anything to save your friend. Tell me the truth. Is that it?

**Mrs Linde** Krogstad, when you've sold yourself once for someone else, you never do it again.

**Krogstad** I will ask for my letter back.

**Mrs Linde** No, you will not.

**Krogstad** I will, yes. I'll stay here till Helmer comes down. I'll insist he give me back my letter. That it's only about my dismissal – he mustn't read it –

**Mrs Linde** You must not ask for your letter back.

**Krogstad** Wasn't that the reason you asked to meet me here?

**Mrs Linde** It was. When I was frightened and didn't know better. Twenty-four hours have passed and in that time I've seen such things in this house that I could not believe. Helmer must be told everything. All this secrecy, this unhappiness, has to end. The two of them must be honest together. No more excuses, and no more evasions.

**Krogstad** As you wish. If you dare to risk this. But one thing I can do and I will do it now –

*Mrs Linde listens.*

**Mrs Linde** Hurry up. Move, go on. The dance is over. We have to leave now.

**Krogstad** I'll wait for you downstairs.

**Mrs Linde** Do. You can walk me to my lodgings.

**Krogstad** I am the happiest man in the whole wide world.

*He exits through the front door. The door between the*

*room and the hall remains open.*

**Mrs Linde** It's happened. (*She tidies up a little and gets her outdoor clothes.*) It's actually happened. Someone to work for, to live for. A home to bring joy to. I can't wait to get started. (*She listens.*) Yes, here they are. I must put on my coat.

> *She puts on her hat and coat. Helmer and Nora's voices are heard in the hall. A key is turned and Helmer leads Nora into the hall, almost by force. She is dressed in the Italian costume, with a big black shawl draped over her shoulders. He is wearing a dinner jacket with a big black cloak. Still in the doorway, Nora resists him.*

**Nora** No, please, not in here, no. I want to go back upstairs. It's too early, I don't want to leave.

**Helmer** My precious Nora, please –

**Nora** I'm begging you, Torvald, I'm begging you please – one hour more, please.

**Helmer** Not one minute more, my sweet Nora. We had an agreement, you know that. Now get into that drawing room or you will catch a chill. (*He leads her gently into the room, despite her resistance.*)

**Mrs Linde** Good evening.

**Nora** Kristine?

**Helmer** Mrs Linde? Are you here so late? Why?

**Mrs Linde** Forgive me, yes. I so wanted to see Nora all dressed up.

**Nora** You've been sitting here waiting for me?

**Mrs Linde** I have. It's a pity I didn't get here in time. You were upstairs already. I didn't think I could leave till I saw you.

*Helmer takes off Nora's shawl.*

**Helmer** Take a good look at her. Do. I would say she's worth looking at. Well, isn't she adorable, Mrs Linde?

**Mrs Linde** Yes, I'd admit –

**Helmer** Isn't she absolutely adorable? The entire party agreed. But she is a Miss Stubbornshoes. The darling creature. What can we do about this? Imagine, I nearly had to drag her out of the room.

**Nora** Torvald, you'll be sorry you didn't let me stay another half an hour.

**Helmer** Do you hear her, Mrs Linde? She dances her tarantella – she brings the house down – and she should have, she should have – though the performance was too much. Too natural. I mean strictly speaking it went beyond the demands of art. Let that pass. What really matters is – she brought the house down. She really did bring the house down. So should I have let her stay after that? Ruin the whole effect? Thank you, no. I took the arm of my lovely little girl from Capri – I should say my wilful little girl from Capri – and we moved through the room so swiftly, a curtsy here, a curtsy there and, as they say in novels, the beautiful vision was no more. An exit should really be an exit, Mrs Linde, but I couldn't make Nora realize that. Dear me, it's so hot in here. (*He throws the cloak on a chair and opens the door to his study.*) It is dark in here. Yes, of course it is. Excuse me.

*He goes in and lights a few candles. Nora whispers quickly and breathlessly.*

**Nora** Well?

*Mrs Linde answers quietly.*

**Mrs Linde** I spoke to him.

**Nora** And?

**Mrs Linde** Nora, tell your husband everything. You have to.

*Nora replies dully.*

**Nora** I knew.

**Mrs Linde** You have nothing to fear where Krogstad's concerned, but you must tell your husband.

**Nora** I won't tell him.

**Mrs Linde** Then the letter will.

**Nora** Thank you Kristine. I know what needs to be done. Ssh.

*Helmer returns.*

**Helmer** Well, Mrs Linde, isn't she adorable?

**Mrs Linde** She is, now I must say goodnight.

**Helmer** So soon? Really? Is that your knitting?

**Mrs Linde** It is, thank you. I nearly forgot it. (*She takes it.*)

**Helmer** So, you knit.

**Mrs Linde** I do.

**Helmer** May I tell you something? Do embroidery instead.

**Mrs Linde** Why is that?

**Helmer** Because it is much more attractive. Watch me. You hold the embroidery in the left, and you move the needle with the right – like this – with grace, perfect grace – isn't that so?

**Mrs Linde** I suppose it is.

**Helmer** But knitting – it's really quite ugly, isn't it? Look at me. Arms all squashed, knitting needles up and down – up and down – there is something Chinese about it. Excellent champagne tonight, they did themselves proud.

**Mrs Linde** Goodnight, Nora, and don't be stubborn any more.

**Helmer** Hear hear, Mrs Linde.

**Mrs Linde** Goodnight, Mr Helmer.

*He accompanies her to the door.*

**Helmer** Goodnight, goodnight. You will get home safely, yes? I would be more than willing to go – but you don't have far to go. Goodnight, goodnight.

*Mrs Linde exits. Helmer closes the door after her and returns.*

Dear God, we've got rid of her at last. That woman, she is extraordinarily boring.

**Nora** Are you worn out, Torvald?

**Helmer** I'm not – no, not at all.

**Nora** Not sleepy even?

**Helmer** I am not. I am wide awake. What about you? Yes, you do look tired and sleepy.

**Nora** I'm worn out, yes. I will sleep soon.

**Helmer** Well, you see I was right not to let you stay any longer.

**Nora** Everything you do is right.

*Helmer kisses Nora's forehead.*

**Helmer** That's my little skylark. Did you see how cheerful Rank was this evening?

84

**Nora** Was he? I didn't say a word to him.

**Helmer** I said a few. But I've not seen him in such good form for a long time. (*He looks at her and moves a little closer.*) It's wonderful to be back at home. To be alone with you. Alone, together. I adore you, you beautiful girl.

**Nora** Don't watch me like that, Torvald.

**Helmer** You're my prize possession, why can't I watch you? Watch the lovely girl who is mine, mine entirely? You're mine.

*Nora goes to the other side of the table.*

**Nora** Don't speak to me like that tonight.

*Helmer follows her.*

**Helmer** Your blood is still dancing the tarantella, I feel it. You are more and more desirable. Do you hear? The guests are starting to leave. Soon the whole house will be quiet. (*He lowers his voice.*)

**Nora** I hope so.

**Helmer** Yes, my beloved, my own Nora. Do you know, when I am at a party with you do you know why I barely breathe a word to you, why I keep my distance, why I steal a glance at you from time to time, do you know why I behave like that? I'm pretending that you're my secret lover, that you're my young, secret fiancée – and no one knows there is anything between us.

**Nora** Yes, I do, I do know. I know all your thoughts are about me.

**Helmer** Then when we leave, and I take the shawl to wrap around your shoulders, around the wonderful curve of your neck, I imagine you're my bride so young, young, we have just been married, I'm taking you to my home, I am alone with you for the first time – alone together, you're trembling, beautiful, young. When I saw you sway and tempt me in the tarantella, my blood was on fire. I could not stand it. That's why I took you with me so early –

**Nora** Go away, Torvald. Leave me. I don't want this.

**Helmer** What? Are you teasing me, Nora? Want – want. I'm your husband.

*A knock is heard on the front door. Nora starts.*

**Nora** Did you hear –

*Helmer calls towards the hall.*

**Helmer** Who is that?

*Rank answers from outside.*

**Rank** It's me. Dare I come in?

*Helmer is quietly annoyed.*

**Helmer** What the hell does he want now? Wait one moment. (*He goes to open the door.*) How thoughtful of you not to pass by our door.

**Rank** I thought I heard your voice and I decided to look in. (*He glances around quickly.*) Yes, these loved, familiar rooms. It's so warm and cosy here with you.

**Helmer** I thought you were very cosy upstairs as well.

**Rank** Very much so. Why shouldn't I be? Why shouldn't one try everything in this life, yes? Try as much as you can, as long as you can. The wine was splendid.

**Helmer** Especially the champagne.

**Rank** You noticed that too? I can barely believe how much I managed to wash down.

**Nora** Torvald drank his fair share of champagne tonight as well.

**Rank** Did he?

**Nora** Yes. And afterwards he is always so jolly.

**Rank** Well, why shouldn't a man enjoy himself after a hard working day?

**Helmer** Hard work? Unfortunately I can't claim that.

*Rank slaps his shoulders.*

**Rank** But I can, you see.

**Nora** Dr Rank, I think you carried out a scientific inquiry today.

**Rank** Spot on. Yes.

**Helmer** Little Nora speaking about scientific inquiries.

**Nora** Should I congratulate you on the result?

**Rank** You should, you should.

**Nora** It went well?

**Rank** The best possible for both doctor and patient – certainty.

*Nora asks quickly and searchingly.*

**Nora** Certainty?

**Rank** Absolute certainty. So shouldn't I allow myself a good evening after that?

**Nora** Yes. You were right to do so, Dr Rank.

**Helmer** I agree. But don't end up suffering the morning after.

**Rank** You get nothing for nothing in this life.

**Nora**  Dr Rank, you do like fancy dress parties?

**Rank**  I do, as long as there are many exotic costumes –

**Nora**  Tell me, what shall we two next dress up as?

**Helmer**  You little silly – are you already thinking of the next ball?

**Rank**  We two? All right, I'll tell you, you shall be the Spirit of Joy –

**Helmer**  But what costume would convey that?

**Rank**  Your wife should appear in her everyday clothes –

**Helmer**  Well put. But what do you want to be?

**Rank**  My good friend, yes, I've no doubt about that.

**Helmer**  Well?

**Rank**  At the next fancy dress, I will be invisible.

**Helmer**  What a strange thought.

**Rank**  There is a big black hat and it makes you invisible. Have you heard of that hat? You put it on and then no one can see you.

*Helmer suppresses a smile.*

**Helmer**  Yes, you are right.

**Rank**  But I'm quite forgetting why I came. Helmer, give me a cigar, one of the black Havanas.

**Helmer**  With pleasure.

*Helmer offers him the box. Rank takes one and cuts off the end.*

**Rank**  Thank you.

*Nora strikes a match.*

**Nora**  Let me light it.

**Rank**  Thank you.

*Nora holds up the match and he lights the cigar.*

And so – goodbye.

**Helmer**  Goodbye, old friend, goodbye.

**Nora**  Sleep well, Dr Rank.

**Rank**  Thank you for your wish.

**Nora**  Wish me the same.

**Rank**  You? If you insist – sleep well. And thank you for the light.

*He nods to both and leaves. Helmer speaks quietly.*

**Helmer**  He's downed a fair amount of drink.

**Nora**  (*absentmindedly*) He may have.

*Helmer takes out his keys and goes to the hall.*

Torvald, what are you doing?

**Helmer**  I have to empty the post box. It's nearly full. There won't be room for tomorrow's papers –

**Nora**  Do you want to work tonight?

**Helmer**  You know very well I don't. What's this? Someone's been at the lock.

**Nora**  The lock?

**Helmer**  Yes. I wouldn't have thought the maids – here's a broken hair pin. It's one of yours, Nora –

*Nora answers quickly.*

**Nora**  It must have been the children –

89

**Helmer** You'll have to tell them never to do that. Anyway, I've managed to open it. (*He takes out the contents and shouts to the kitchen.*) Helene, put out the lamp in the hall. (*He enters the living room and closes the door to the hall. He stands with the letters in his hand.*) Do you see how they've piled up. (*He leafs through the pile.*) What is this?

*Nora is by the window.*

**Nora** The letter. No, Torvald, no.

**Helmer** Two visiting cards from Rank.

**Nora** From Dr Rank?

*Helmer looks at them.*

**Helmer** Rank, Doctor of Medicine. They were at the top. He must have dropped these in as he was leaving.

**Nora** Do they say anything?

**Helmer** A black cross above his name – look. What an appalling idea. It's as if he's announcing his own death.

**Nora** He is.

**Helmer** Do you know something? Has he told you something?

**Nora** When the cards come, he is saying goodbye to us. He wants to lock himself away and die.

**Helmer** My poor friend. I knew I wouldn't have him much longer. But so soon. And he hides himself away like a wounded animal.

**Nora** If it has to happen, then it's best to let it happen in silence. Isn't that so, Torvald?

*Helmer paces the room.*

**Helmer**  He was a part of us. I can't imagine him gone. His suffering, his loneliness were like a cloudy background to the sunlight of our happiness. Perhaps it is for the best like this. For him at any rate. (*He stops.*) For us too, perhaps, Nora. Now we're quite dependent on each other. (*He throws his arms around Nora.*) Darling, how can I hold you tightly enough? Nora, do you know that I've often wished you were facing some terrible dangers so that I could risk life and limb, risk everything, for your sake?

*Nora tears herself away and speaks in a strong, determined voice.*

**Nora**  Read your letters. Now, Torvald.

**Helmer**  Not tonight. No. I want to be with you, my darling wife.

**Nora**  Your friend's dying – think of him.

**Helmer**  Yes, you're right. This has upset the two of us. This ugly thing has come between us. Death and decay. We should clear our minds of that. Until then, we will go to our separate rooms.

*Nora is around his neck.*

**Nora**  Goodnight, Torvald, goodnight.

*Helmer kisses her on the forehead.*

**Helmer**  Goodnight, my little singing bird. Sleep well, Nora. I'm going to read all these letters from beginning to end.

*He goes with the bundle in his hand into his study and closes the door behind him. With despair in her eyes, Nora fumbles about, gets hold of Helmer's cloak, throws it about herself, whispering quickly, brokenly, hoarsely.*

**Nora** I will never see him again. Never. Never. Never. (*She throws her shawl over her head.*) Children, never see them again. Not them either. Never. The black, cold, icy water. Down and down, without end – if it would only end. Now he's got it. Now he's reading it. No. Not yet. Torvald, goodbye and children –

*She is about to rush through the hall. At the same time Helmer throws open his door and stands with an opened letter in his hand.*

**Helmer** Nora.

*She screams loudly.*

What is this? Do you know what's written in this letter?

**Nora** I know. Let me go. Let me leave.

*He holds her back.*

**Helmer** Where are you going?

**Nora** Torvald, don't save me.

*He staggers back.*

**Helmer** Is what he writes true? It's horrible. It can't possibly be true.

**Nora** It's all true. I've loved you more than anything in this world –

**Helmer** Don't give me your pathetic excuses.

*She takes a step towards him.*

**Nora** Torvald –

**Helmer** You pathetic fool, do you know what you've done?

**Nora** Let me leave. You're not going to suffer for my sake. You're not going to take the blame.

**Helmer** Stop play-acting. (*He locks the door.*) You will explain here and now. Do you understand what you've done? Answer me. Do you understand what you've done?

*Nora looks at him steadily and answers with a frozen expression.*

**Nora** Yes. Now I'm beginning to understand.

*Helmer paces the floor.*

**Helmer** I've really had my eyes opened. In all these years. You who were my pride and joy, a hypocrite! A liar! Worse . . . a criminal! The ugliness of it all.

*Nora is silent. She stares at him without blinking. Helmer stops in front of her.*

I should have known something like this would happen. Your father was a reckless man and you are his reckless daughter – don't interrupt. No religion, no morals, no sense of duty. I'm being punished for closing my eyes to his faults. I did it for your sake. This is how you repay me.

**Nora** Yes, this is how.

**Helmer** Now you've ruined my happiness. You've thrown away my whole future. I am at the mercy of a man with no conscience. He can do as he likes with me, demand what he wants from me, he can bully and command me as he pleases. I daren't complain. I will have to sink, I'm going under because of you, woman.

**Nora** When I'm out of the way, you'll be free.

**Helmer** Spare me your dramatic gestures. Your father was always ready with that kind of talk. You, out of the way? How in the hell would that help me? He can let this whole business be known anyway. If he does, then I might be suspected of aiding and abetting your crime. People might think I was behind it – that I encouraged you. And it's you I can thank for all of this. You that I carried with my two hands throughout our entire marriage. Do you understand what you've done to me?

*Nora is calmly cold.*

**Nora**  I do.

**Helmer**  That's what is so unbelievable. That, I can't take in. Still, we must deal with it. Take off your shawl. Take it off, I say. I must try to satisfy him in some way. This has to be kept quiet at any price. And as far as we're concerned, we must look as if nothing has changed. But only in public. From now on you will stay in the house. But you won't be allowed to bring up the children. I daren't trust you with them. To have to say this to the woman I loved and still – But that's all over. From now on, forget happiness. Now it's just about saving the remains, the wreckage, the appearance.

*The front door bell rings. Helmer starts.*

What is it? It's late. Could it be the worst? Would he –? Nora, hide, say you're sick!

*She stands without moving as Helmer goes to open the door to the hall. The Maid, half dressed, appears in the doorway.*

**Maid**  A letter, Madam. Addressed to you.

**Helmer**  Give me it. (*He grasps the letter and closes the door.*) It's from him, yes. You won't get it. I'll read it myself.

**Nora**  You read it.

*Helmer is by the lamp.*

**Helmer**  We may be ruined, you and me. (*He tears open*

94

*the letter in a hurry, reads it, looks at an enclosed paper and gives a cry of joy.)* Nora.

*Nora looks at him inquisitively.*

Nora. I must read it again. Yes. Yes. It's true. I'm saved. Nora, I'm saved. I am.

**Nora**  And me?

**Helmer**  You too, naturally. We're both saved, you and me. Look. Your contract, he's returning it. He regrets, he repents, he says. His life has turned for the better – who cares what he says? Nora, we're saved. No one can harm you. Nora. Nora, let's get rid of this hideous thing. *(He glances at the paper.)* I won't look at it. A bad dream, that's all it's been. *(He tears the contract, both letters, into pieces. He throws everything into the stove and watches it burn.)* There. They don't exist any more. He says that since Christmas Eve, you – they must have been three dreadful days for you, Nora.

**Nora**  I fought a hard battle these past three days.

**Helmer**  And you tortured yourself, you could see no way out but to – No, we won't remember ugliness. We'll be happy and we'll keep saying, it's finished, it's finished. Listen to me, Nora, you don't seem to understand. It's finished. Now what's this – this cold expression? Dear little Nora, I do know. You just can't believe that I've forgiven you everything. I do know that what you did you did out of love for me.

**Nora**  That's true.

**Helmer**  A wife should love her husband, and that's how you love me. But the ends didn't justify the means in this case, and you didn't have the knowledge to realize that. Do you think I love you less because you don't know how to act on your own? No. Lean on me. I'll advise you. I'll teach you. I wouldn't be much of a man if your being helpless didn't make you doubly attractive. Don't pay any heed to my harsh words earlier. I was frightened then. I thought everything would collapse on top of me. I've forgiven you, Nora. I swear to you I've forgiven you.

**Nora** Thank you for your forgiveness. (*She exits through the door, stage right.*)

**Helmer** Don't go – (*He looks in.*) What are you up to in your room?

*Nora speaks off-stage.*

**Nora** Taking off my fancy dress.

*Helmer is by the open door.*

**Helmer** Do that, yes. Then calm down and collect your thoughts, my frightened singing bird. You can rest now. I have big wings to cover you. (*He paces close to the door.*) Our home is so cosy, so lovely, Nora. There's shelter for you here. I'll watch over you. I've saved you from the hawk's claws, and they've hunted you, you poor dove. Your heart's beating, I'll calm it. It will happen bit by bit. Nora, believe me – tomorrow everything will look quite different to you. Everything will soon be like it was before. I'll have no need to tell you I forgive you. You'll feel yourself that it's certain I have. How could you even think I could dismiss you and even blame you for anything? You don't know what a real heart – a man's heart is, Nora. How can I describe it? There is something so sweet, so satisfying for a man to know in himself that he has forgiven his wife. He's forgiven her from the bottom of his heart. It's as if he's twice made her his own. It's like he's given her a new life. In a way she has become his wife and his child. From now on that's what you'll be for me. You bewildered, helpless, little creature. Nora, don't be frightened of anything. Whatever you need, tell me. I will be your strength and your conscience. What's this? Not gone to bed? Have you changed?

*Nora is in her day clothes.*

**Nora**  Yes, Torvald, I've changed now.

**Helmer**  But it's so late – why?

**Nora**  I won't sleep tonight.

**Helmer**  But Nora, my dear –

*Nora looks at her watch.*

**Nora**  It's not very late yet. Torvald, sit down. The two of us have a lot to say to each other. (*She sits down on one side of the table.*)

**Helmer**  What is this Nora? You're looking so coldly at me –

**Nora**  Sit down, this will take a long time. I have so much to say to you.

*Helmer sits at the other side of the table.*

**Helmer**  You worry me, Nora. I don't understand you.

**Nora**  No. That's just it. You do not understand me. I have never understood you either. Until tonight. Do not interrupt me. Listen to me. Torvald, it is time to be honest.

**Helmer**  What do you mean?

*There is a short pause.*

**Nora**  Does anything strike you about the way we're sitting here?

**Helmer**  What?

**Nora**  We've been married now for eight years. This is the first time the two of us, you and me, man and wife, are having a serious conversation.

**Helmer**  What do you mean serious?

**Nora**  For eight whole years – longer even – from the first day we met, we have never exchanged one serious word about serious things.

**Helmer**  So I should have shared worries that you could never have helped me with anyway?

**Nora**  I'm not talking about worries. I'm saying that we have never sat down and seriously tried to get to the heart of anything.

**Helmer**  Would you have liked that, Nora?

**Nora**  That's the point. You've never understood me. I've been wronged, Torvald, and badly so. First by Papa and then by you.

**Helmer**  What? Us? The two who have loved you more than anyone else?

*Nora shakes her head.*

**Nora**  You never loved me. You just thought it was enjoyable to be in love with me.

**Helmer**  What are you saying, Nora?

**Nora**  The truth, Torvald. At home with Papa he told me his opinions about everything, and I had the same opinions. If I thought differently, I hid it. Because he wouldn't have liked it. He called me his little doll, and he played with me the same way I played with my dolls. Then I came to your house –

**Helmer**  What kind of expression is that to use about our marriage?

*Nora is undisturbed.*

**Nora** I was handed from Papa to you. You organized everything according to your taste, and I picked up the same taste as you. Or I just pretended to. I don't really know. I think I did both. First one, then the other. When I look back at it now, it seems to me that I have been living like a beggar, from hand to mouth. I have been performing tricks for you, Torvald. That's how I've survived. You wanted it like that. You and Papa have done me a great wrong. It's because of you I've made nothing of my life.

**Helmer** That's not rational, Nora, and it's not grateful. Have you not been happy here?

**Nora** No, I have never been happy here. I thought I was, but I never was.

**Helmer** Not happy? Never –

**Nora** No. Just cheerful. And you were always kind to me. But our home was just a playroom. Here, where I've been your doll-wife, the way I was Papa's doll-child. The children, they became my dolls. I thought it was fun when you played with me, Torvald, the same way they thought it fun when I played with them. Our marriage, Torvald, that is what it's been.

**Helmer** There is some truth in what you say, even if it is exaggerated and hysterical. But from now on things will change. Playtime is over. It's time for teaching.

**Nora** Who will be taught? Me or the children?

**Helmer** Both you and the children, Nora my love.

**Nora** Torvald, you are not the man to teach me how to be the proper wife for you.

**Helmer** How can you say that?

**Nora**  And me – how am I equipped to teach the children?

**Helmer**  Nora.

**Nora**  Didn't you say that to me just now? You didn't dare trust me with them.

**Helmer**  In a moment of anger. Why take notice of that?

**Nora**  Because what you said was true. I'm not equipped for it. I must do something else first. I must educate myself. You are not the man to help me with that. I have to do it on my own. That's why I'm leaving you now.

*Helmer jumps up.*

**Helmer**  What did you say?

**Nora**  I must stand on my own if I'm to make sense of myself and everything around me. That's why I can't live with you any longer.

**Helmer**  Nora, Nora.

**Nora**  I'll leave now. Kristine will put me up for tonight.

**Helmer**  You are mad. I won't allow you. I forbid you.

**Nora**  It's no use forbidding me anything any more. I'll take what is mine with me. I want nothing from you now or ever again.

**Helmer**  What kind of lunacy is this?

**Nora**  I'm going home tomorrow, to my old home, I mean. It will be easier for me to find something to do there.

**Helmer**  You can't see what you're doing, you have no experience.

**Nora**  Then I must get experience, Torvald.

**Helmer**  Abandon your home, your husband, your children? What do you think people will say?

**Nora** I can't take any notice of that. I just know what I must do.

**Helmer** This is monstrous. Can you abandon your most sacred duties like this?

**Nora** What do you think my most sacred duties are?

**Helmer** Do I need to tell you that? You have a duty to your husband and your children, don't you?

**Nora** I have other duties that are just as sacred.

**Helmer** No, you haven't. What duties are those?

**Nora** My duties to myself.

**Helmer** You are a wife and a mother before everything else.

**Nora** I don't believe that any more. I believe that I am a human being, just as much as you are – or at least I will try to become one. I know most people would agree with you, Torvald. And books say things like that. But I am not satisfied now with what most people say or with what it says in books. I need to think about these things for myself and find out about them.

**Helmer** Don't you understand your place in your own home? Don't you have an infallible guide? Haven't you got religion?

**Nora** Torvald, I don't even know what religion is.

**Helmer** What are you saying?

**Nora** I only know what Pastor Hansen told me when I was confirmed. He said religion meant this and that. When I am away from all of this, when I'm on my own, I'll think over this too. I want to see if what Pastor Hansen told me was right, or at least if it's right for me.

**Helmer** This is unheard of coming from a young woman. But if you reject religion, what about your conscience? Are you still in touch with any morality? Or maybe you have none. Answer me.

**Nora** It's not easy to answer that, Torvald. I don't know really. I'm very confused about those things. But I do know I look at them differently from you. I now find out the law differs from what I'd imagined. I simply can't believe that the law should be right. A woman is not allowed to spare her old, dying father, or to save her husband's life – I don't believe that.

**Helmer** You're talking like a child. You don't understand the society you live in.

**Nora** I don't, no. But now I'm about to find out. I must find out who's right – society or me.

**Helmer** You're ill, Nora. You're feverish. I almost think you've taken leave of your senses.

**Nora** I've never felt so clear and certain as tonight.

**Helmer** So clear and certain that you leave your husband and children?

**Nora** I do, yes.

**Helmer** There's only one way to explain this.

**Nora** What?

**Helmer** You don't love me any more.

**Nora** That's just it.

**Helmer** Nora, how can you say that?

**Nora** It hurts me very much, Torvald, because you have always been so generous to me. But I can't help it. I do not love you any more.

*Helmer forces self-control.*

**Helmer** And are you clear and certain of that too?

**Nora** Yes, absolutely clear, absolutely certain. That's why I don't want to stay here any more.

**Helmer** Can you tell me how I lost your love?

**Nora** Yes, I can. It was tonight, when something glorious didn't happen, because then I saw you were not the man I thought you were.

**Helmer** Explain yourself. I don't understand you.

**Nora** I've been patiently waiting for eight years, because God knows I do realize something glorious doesn't happen every day. Then this dreadful blow hit me, and I was utterly certain that now something glorious would happen. When Krogstad's letter lay out there, I never thought you would accept that man's conditions. I was so utterly certain of what you would say to him. Tell the truth to the whole world. And when that happened –

**Helmer** What then? When I'd exposed my wife to shame and humiliation –

**Nora** When that had happened, I believed with such utter certainty that you would step forward, you would take the blame, you would say, 'I am the guilty one'.

**Helmer** Nora –

**Nora** You believe I would never have allowed such a sacrifice from you. No, of course not. But what would what I have to say count against what you had to say? That was the glorious thing I hoped for and feared. And to stop that happening I wanted to end my life.

**Helmer** Nora, for you I would have worked day and night. For your sake I would have suffered any sorrow or hardship. But no man sacrifices his integrity for the person he loves.

**Nora** Hundreds of thousands of women have.

**Helmer** You're thinking and speaking like an ignorant child.

**Nora** Be that as it may, but you don't think or speak like a man I can share my life with. When you stopped being frightened, it was not of what was threatening me: you were frightened of what you had to face. When you stopped being frightened, it was as if nothing had happened. I was your little singing bird just like before. Your doll that you would carry now with twice the care, since it was so weak and fragile. (*She gets up.*) Torvald, at that moment, I realized I'd lived with a stranger for eight years and that I'd borne him three children – I can't bear to think of it. It tears me to pieces.

*Helmer speaks sadly.*

**Helmer** I see now. I see. There's a big gap between us. Yes. Nora, can we not reach across it?

**Nora** The way I am now, I am no wife to you.

**Helmer** I have the strength to be another man.

**Nora** Perhaps – if your doll is taken from you.

**Helmer** Separated – separated from you? No, Nora, I can't bear that thought.

*Nora goes to the room, stage right.*

**Nora** That makes it all the more necessary that we do it. (*She returns with her coat and a small bag which she puts on the chair by the table.*)

**Helmer** Nora, not now. Wait till tomorrow, Nora.

*Nora puts on her coat.*

**Nora**  I can't spend the night in a stranger's house.

**Helmer**  Can we not live here as brother and sister –?

**Nora**  You know very well that wouldn't last long. (*She wraps the shawl around herself.*) Goodbye, Torvald. I don't want to see the children. They're in better hands than mine, I'm sure. I can be no use to them, the way I am now.

**Helmer**  But some day, Nora, some day –

**Nora**  How do I know? I don't even know what will happen to me.

**Helmer**  But you're my wife, you are now, you always will be.

**Nora**  Listen, Torvald, when a wife walks out of her husband's house, as I'm walking out now, to the best of my knowledge the law frees him completely from her. In any case, I'm freeing you completely. Don't feel you're tied in any way, no more than I will be. We both must be completely free. Look, here's your ring. Give me mine.

**Helmer**  That as well?

**Nora**  That as well.

**Helmer**  Here it is.

**Nora**  Yes, now it is finished. I will put my keys here. The maids know everything about the house – better than I do. Tomorrow, when I've gone, Kristine will come here and pack the things that I've brought from home. I will have them sent on to me.

**Helmer**  Finished, finished. Will you ever think of me, Nora?

**Nora**  I'll think of you often and of the children and the house here.

**Helmer**  Nora, can I write to you?

**Nora**  No – never. I won't allow you that.

**Helmer**  At least can I send you –

**Nora**  Nothing. Nothing.

**Helmer**  Let me help you, if you need it.

**Nora**  No. I'm telling you I take nothing from strangers.

**Helmer**  Can I never be anything but a stranger to you, Nora?

*Nora takes her bag.*

**Nora**  Torvald, then something glorious would have to happen –

**Helmer**  What is this something glorious?

**Nora**  You and I would both have to change so much that – Torvald, I no longer believe in something glorious.

**Helmer**  But I want to believe in it. Say it. Change so much that –

**Nora**  That our marriage could become a life together. Goodbye.

*She exits through the hall. Helmer sinks down in a chair by the door and buries his face in his hands.*

**Helmer**  Nora, Nora. (*He looks around and gets up.*) Empty. She is not here any more. (*A hope rises in him.*) Something glorious –

*Downstairs the street door slams shut.*